Korea: A Very Short Introduction

VERY SHORT INTRODUCTIONS are for anyone wanting a stimulating and accessible way into a new subject. They are written by experts, and have been translated into more than 45 different languages.

The series began in 1995, and now covers a wide variety of topics in every discipline. The VSI library currently contains over 600 volumes—a Very Short Introduction to everything from Psychology and Philosophy of Science to American History and Relativity—and continues to grow in every subject area.

Very Short Introductions available now:

ABOLITIONISM Richard S. Newman
THE ABRAHAMIC RELIGIONS
    Charles L. Cohen
ACCOUNTING Christopher Nobes
ADAM SMITH Christopher J. Berry
ADOLESCENCE Peter K. Smith
ADVERTISING Winston Fletcher
AESTHETICS Bence Nanay
AFRICAN AMERICAN
    RELIGION Eddie S. Glaude Jr
AFRICAN HISTORY John Parker and
    Richard Rathbone
AFRICAN POLITICS Ian Taylor
AFRICAN RELIGIONS
    Jacob K. Olupona
AGEING Nancy A. Pachana
AGNOSTICISM Robin Le Poidevin
AGRICULTURE Paul Brassley and
    Richard Soffe
ALEXANDER THE GREAT
    Hugh Bowden
ALGEBRA Peter M. Higgins
AMERICAN CULTURAL HISTORY
    Eric Avila
AMERICAN FOREIGN RELATIONS
    Andrew Preston
AMERICAN HISTORY Paul S. Boyer
AMERICAN IMMIGRATION
    David A. Gerber
AMERICAN LEGAL HISTORY
    G. Edward White
AMERICAN NAVAL HISTORY
    Craig L. Symonds
AMERICAN POLITICAL HISTORY
    Donald Critchlow

AMERICAN POLITICAL PARTIES
    AND ELECTIONS L. Sandy Maisel
AMERICAN POLITICS
    Richard M. Valelly
THE AMERICAN PRESIDENCY
    Charles O. Jones
THE AMERICAN REVOLUTION
    Robert J. Allison
AMERICAN SLAVERY
    Heather Andrea Williams
THE AMERICAN WEST Stephen Aron
AMERICAN WOMEN'S HISTORY
    Susan Ware
ANAESTHESIA Aidan O'Donnell
ANALYTIC PHILOSOPHY
    Michael Beaney
ANARCHISM Colin Ward
ANCIENT ASSYRIA Karen Radner
ANCIENT EGYPT Ian Shaw
ANCIENT EGYPTIAN ART AND
    ARCHITECTURE Christina Riggs
ANCIENT GREECE Paul Cartledge
THE ANCIENT NEAR EAST
    Amanda H. Podany
ANCIENT PHILOSOPHY Julia Annas
ANCIENT WARFARE
    Harry Sidebottom
ANGELS David Albert Jones
ANGLICANISM Mark Chapman
THE ANGLO-SAXON AGE John Blair
ANIMAL BEHAVIOUR
    Tristram D. Wyatt
THE ANIMAL KINGDOM
    Peter Holland
ANIMAL RIGHTS David DeGrazia

Available soon:

For more information visit our website

www.oup.com/vsi/

Michael J. Seth

KOREA

A Very Short Introduction

OXFORD
UNIVERSITY PRESS

OXFORD

UNIVERSITY PRESS

Great Clarendon Street, Oxford, OX2 6DP,
United Kingdom

Oxford University Press is a department of the University of Oxford.
It furthers the University's objective of excellence in research, scholarship,
and education by publishing worldwide. Oxford is a registered trade mark of
Oxford University Press in the UK and in certain other countries

© Michael J. Seth 2020

The moral rights of the author have been asserted

First edition published in 2020

All rights reserved. No part of this publication may be reproduced, stored in
a retrieval system, or transmitted, in any form or by any means, without the
prior permission in writing of Oxford University Press, or as expressly permitted
by law, by licence or under terms agreed with the appropriate reprographics
rights organization. Enquiries concerning reproduction outside the scope of the
above should be sent to the Rights Department, Oxford University Press, at the
address above

You must not circulate this work in any other form
and you must impose this same condition on any acquirer

Published in the United States of America by Oxford University Press
198 Madison Avenue, New York, NY 10016, United States of America

British Library Cataloguing in Publication Data
Data available

Library of Congress Control Number: 2019949430

ISBN 978-0-19-883077-1

Printed and bound by
CPI Group (UK) Ltd, Croydon, CR0 4YY

Contents

List of illustrations

List of maps

Introduction

Korea, long in the shadows of its neighbours China and Japan, is now the object of considerable interest for radically different reasons—the South as an economic success story and for its vibrant popular culture; the North as the home to one of the world's most repressive regimes, at once both bizarre and menacing. This book hopes to encourage and inform this growing interest in Korea by introducing its history. Since there is so much to tell in such a short book it focuses on several historical questions: what does it mean to be Korean; how did the various peoples of the Korean peninsula become a single nation; how did this nation evolve, in a single lifetime, into today's sharply contrasting societies; and how does Korea fit into the larger narrative of world history?

Koreans today see themselves as an ethnically, racially, linguistically, and culturally homogeneous people, unnaturally divided into two halves. They take pride in this homogeneity and in being part of a unique nation with a long history dating back several millennia. There is some basis for this belief about themselves. Virtually all people of the modern states of North and South Korea speak the same Korean language, a language which appears to be unrelated to any other living tongue. It is written in its own distinct alphabet quite different from other writing systems. Both Koreas are, or have been until very recently, among the most ethnically uniform societies in the world. And contemporary Korea is the inheritor of a long cultural tradition that can be traced back many centuries.

However, the historical basis for the modern sense of national identity is open to question or at least qualification. Korea as a 'country' dates only to the Late Silla kingdom of the 7th century, and even then it was not the only state on the peninsula. The present political boundaries of Korea (when North and South are considered together) date only from the 15th century. This still makes it among the oldest and least changed countries in the world. Least changed on the map, that is; in other ways modern Korea has shown a capacity to transform itself with astounding rapidity. This is one of its most fascinating characteristics.

This book presents a chronological history of Korea defined as the people and states that have existed within or mostly within the boundaries of North and South Korea. The first two chapters cover the pre-modern period, that is, the period up to the 19th century. The third covers the beginning of Korea's modern transformation during the last decades of the dynastic state and during the period of Japanese colonial rule. The fourth chapter begins at the close of the Second World War and ends with the termination of the Korean War, when the division of Korea into two states became a long-term reality. The last two chapters examine the radically different trajectories of North and South Korea since 1953.

Geographic setting

The two Koreas today—the Democratic People's Republic of Korea (DPRK or North Korea) and the Republic of Korea (ROK or South Korea)—occupy two halves of the former dynastic Korean state that lost its independence in 1910. Both states see themselves as the sole legitimate heir of this historical state.

Even when the two Koreas are viewed as a single country, as most Koreans do, it looks small on the map compared to its neighbours China and Russia. But it is a medium-sized country. The area that makes up the two Koreas today is 600 miles (1000 km) from north to south, averaging about 120 miles (200 km) in width. Its size and length are about the same as Great Britain, a little smaller and shorter than Italy. North Korea is slightly larger in area, 46,000 square miles (122,000 sq km) compared to the 38,000 square miles (99,000 sq km) of South Korea. Most of Korea lies on a peninsula bordered on the north by China and a corner of Russia, and on three sides by the sea. While seas surrounding the peninsula make for a natural boundary, the northernmost part of the country has historically not been so well defined. Its current borders, formed six centuries ago, are delineated by Paektu Mountain, a 9,003-foot (2,744 m) volcano and the two rivers that flow from it: the Tumen River that heads north-east and empties into the East Sea (Sea of Japan) and the Yalu River that flows south-west to the Yellow Sea.

Koreans have called themselves a 'shrimp among whales', meaning they are a small country surrounded by much bigger ones: China, Russia, Japan, and in the past great continental empires such as that of the Mongols. Today Korea is bordered by China's north-east region of Manchuria although through most of its history this region was not Chinese, but part of the steppe and forest lands of the north-east, home to some of the world's most formidable warrior peoples. However, China was close enough to be the inspiration for many of Korea's ideas about government, society, art, literature, and religion. To the south-east, the 115-mile (185 km) Korea Strait separates the peninsula from the Japanese archipelago, just wide enough to make these very different lands yet narrow enough to ensure frequent interaction. In fact, Korea has often been a bridge between the mainland and Japan.

Over three-quarters of Korea is covered by mountains. The principal chain, the T'aebaek Range, covers most of the north-east

3

and runs like a central spine along the eastern part of the country with smaller ranges branching off it. The mountains are not high: Paektu is the highest, and the tallest in South Korea reaches only 6,388 feet (1,947 m); however, they are rugged enough to hamper trans-regional trade and communication. Cultivatable land is limited, yet is fertile, well watered, and capable of high crop yields. The north-east has long severe winters, but the central and southern areas have shorter winters and a longer growing season. The seas around Korea are rich in fish, squid, and other ocean products. Therefore, although it is small and mountainous, Korea has been able to support large populations. Today fifty million people live in South Korea and twenty-five million in North Korea.

A note on Romanization

Modern Korean is written in the Korean alphabet Hangul (*han'gŭl*). There are two forms of Romanization of the complex sound system of Korean in wide use: McCune-Reischauer, and the newer one officially adopted by the South Korean government in 2000, Revised Romanization. They are very different. For example, the common names for Korea written Chosŏn and Koryŏ in McCune-Reischauer are written Joseon and Goryeo in Revised Romanization. While Revised Romanization has been gaining acceptance, this book follows the McCune-Reischauer system that with minor variations is still used in most scholarly literature. In some cases when a person or thing is more widely known by a different spelling this book uses that one. For example, instead of Pak Chŏnghŭi, the South Korean president's name is written as Park Chung Hee, the way it more commonly appears.

Chapter 1
Creating a peninsular kingdom

Koreans are fond of saying that they have 5,000 years of history: a rather arbitrary designation. If by Korean history what is meant is the story of a nation or a people who possessed a common sense of being Korean, then 5,000 years is far too long. The first state to occupy most of the peninsula did not appear until the 7th century CE and it was centuries later before a shared identity among the inhabitants of the peninsula emerged. If, however, Korean history is understood to be the history of the people in what comprises the area of the two Koreas today, then it is far too short, for evidence of human activity in Korea dates back tens of thousands of years (Map 1, Map 2).

The 5,000 years is based on the Tan'gun, the mythical founder of the first Korean state. According to the story first recorded in the 13th century, Tan'gun was the offspring of a celestial deity and a she-bear. Born on a mountain today associated with Paektu Mountain, Tan'gun is honoured in both Koreas. In the North, stripped of some of the supernatural elements he is taught as a real historical person who founded the first Korean state. His tomb was 'discovered' and is a tourist sight. In the South, while the story of Tan'gun is taught as a myth, there is a holiday in his honour. For Korean nationalists, North and South, he symbolizes the uniqueness and the antiquity of the Korean people, and the autonomous nature of their historical development.

Map 1. Map of Korea.

Map 2. Map of East Asia.

There is another myth associated with the creation of early Korea—the story of Kija. A relative of the last emperor of the Shang Dynasty of China, Kija fled China to the peninsula when the dynasty fell in 1122 BCE. There he introduced agriculture, literature, and all the refinements of civilization to the Korean people. He went on to become ruler of the Korean state of Chosŏn. Although many pre-modern Korean historians began their histories with Kija, in modern times Korean nationalists were uncomfortable with the Kija myth since it suggested that Korean culture was derivative rather than original, and subservient to outsiders rather than independent. The myth, however, reflects the importance of China in shaping that culture.

Early Korean societies

About 6,000 years ago people in Korea began cultivating millet and raising pigs. By 3,000 years ago they began growing rice, probably introduced from China. Rice grows well in the soils and climate of Korea. It is planted in the spring, matures during the hot, rainy summer, and ripens in the dry, sunny autumn. It has been the basic staple of the Korean diet for all of its recorded history. It is not possible to link early farming cultures with any ethnic or linguistic group. In fact, it is difficult to say when a distinctively 'Korean culture' emerges. The cultures of ancient Korea overlap with those of lands around it forming a broader, fluctuating, north-east Asian cultural zone. The earliest pottery dating from 10,000 years ago is similar to pottery found in much of north-east Asia and western Japan. Bronze artefacts such as daggers and multi-knobbed mirrors which appeared less than 3,000 years ago resemble those in adjacent parts of Manchuria and parts of northern China. This is also true of the megaliths. Erected during the last millennium BCE these were modest in size—nothing on the scale of Stonehenge—but numerous; thousands have been discovered, far more than in all of Europe. While there were two distinctive regional styles, one in southern Korea and one in northern Korea, both were part of the larger area of megaliths encompassing Manchuria, northern Shandong province in China, and northern Kyushu in Japan.

Around 300 BCE, Chinese sources began referring to a Chaoxian kingdom (Korean: Chosŏn), called Old Chosŏn by modern Korean historians to distinguish it from the later Chosŏn dynasty that ended in 1910. Chosŏn (also written Joseon) is one of the names

Koreans have used for their country and is the common term for 'Korea' used in North Korea. Little is known about Old Chosŏn, which may have been more of a tribal confederation than a state. Even its location is not certain other than its last capital Wanggŏm, which was located at the site of modern Pyongyang (P'yŏngyang). The last ruler, Ugŏ, who is the first person in Korean history that is more historical than mythical, incurred the wrath of the Emperor Wudi of China by blocking Chinese trade with the tribal peoples of the area. Wudi sent his army in and conquered the Old Chosŏn in 109–108 BCE, an event that also gives us the first firm date in Korean history.

For the next four centuries parts of northern Korea became incorporated into the Chinese Empire. It was a remote outpost whose most important centre was in the vicinity of modern Pyongyang. From there the Chinese conducted trade and diplomacy with the tribal peoples of Korea, Manchuria, and Japan, or, as the Chinese referred to them, the 'eastern barbarians'. For the peoples of Korea, the Chinese presence in the north-east served as an important conduit for Chinese culture, and ideas of political and social organization.

By the 3rd century CE Chinese records provide descriptions of the tribal peoples of Korea. The most important of these were the Koguryŏ and the Han. The Koguryŏ originally lived in Manchuria north of the Yalu River but gradually moved south raiding northern Korea while stirring up trouble for the Chinese in the process. The Han divided into three groups: the Mahan, Chinhan, and Pyŏnghan lived in the area of what is now South Korea. All appear to have spoken the same language, which most scholars believe was ancestral to modern Korean. Indeed, Koreans today, especially in the South, see themselves as their direct descendants, calling themselves the Han. Han'guk (Han Country) is one of the common names for Korea and it is the official name used in South Korea.

The tribal peoples of Korea gradually coalesced into states, although the process is poorly recorded and not well understood. In the 3rd century the Chinese Empire went into decline and by the 4th century was unable to sustain a presence in Korea. In the political vacuum that followed three indigenous states emerged that dominated Korea from the 4th to the 7th century: Koguryŏ in the north, Paekche in the south-west, and Silla (pronounced Shilla) in the south-east. Paekche and Silla appear in the historical record in the 4th century; Koguryŏ began its transition from a tribal federation to a state earlier (Figure 1). There were also six tiny polities referred to collectively as Kaya but these were absorbed by Silla. Another possible presence in Korea at this time were the Wa, as the ancient peoples of Japan were called by the Chinese.

The retreat of China's political authority did not end the flow of Chinese cultural influence into the peninsula. Buddhist monks from China converted the rulers of the three states which adopted

1. **Hunting scene, *Tomb of the Dancers*, Koguryŏ, *c*.5th century** CE.

Buddhism as a royal protective cult. Koguryŏ, Paekche, and Silla carried on religious, diplomatic, and trade exchanges with the various states on the Chinese mainland and modelled their bureaucracy and legal systems on them. Each used Chinese for record keeping. Despite the growing influence of Chinese culture each of the Three Kingdoms was ruled by warrior-aristocrats, mounted archers whose lifestyles showed affinity to the peoples of Manchuria and Inner Asia, from which the ruling classes probably descended (Map 3). Koguryŏ, the largest of the three kingdoms at

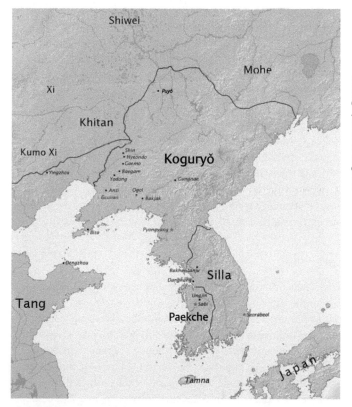

Map 3. Map of the Three Kingdoms.

its peak, covered most of southern Manchuria, North Korea, and the area around modern Seoul. From its base in the Yalu River basin, it expanded southward into the area around Pyongyang, where it relocated its capital. Paekche, centred in the rich agricultural lands in south-west Korea, was a more urbanized and literate society than its rougher warrior neighbour to the north. Nonetheless, its ruling family claimed Manchurian origins and was dominated by a warrior-aristocracy that wore armour, rode horses, and were skilled bowmen.

Much of Korea's pre-modern history was shaped by its interaction with China, not just culturally but politically; and it was China's intervention in the peninsula that precipitated the unification of most of the peninsula. For two and a half centuries the three Korean kingdoms fought each other for supremacy. In 589 China was reunified under the Sui dynasty. The Sui and the Tang dynasty, which succeeded it in 618, worked toward securing their border areas. This included the elimination of Koguryŏ, which Tang achieved with Silla help. First the Tang imperial government supported Silla's conquest of Paekche in 660, and then carried out a joint invasion of Koguryŏ. Following Koguryŏ's fall, the Chinese rulers attempted to make Silla into a client state under their control, but instead Silla drove the Chinese out of the peninsula in 676. There was now a single state in Korea.

Late Silla

When Silla drove out the Chinese in 676 it absorbed Paekche and the southernmost parts of Koguryŏ. South Koreans often refer to this as the 'unification of Korea' under Silla. According to many accounts of Korean history, Silla was followed by two changes of dynasties; each time the kingdom would be renamed: first Koryŏ in the 10th century, and then Chosŏn in the late 14th. Still it was essentially the same state, whose demise came only in 1910 when it fell under Japanese rule. After thirty-five years as a Japanese colony Korea would be divided by the Soviet Union and the United States in 1945. The two states North and South Korea that emerged in 1948 can be seen as successors to the original dynastic state created by Silla.

There are problems with this common interpretation of history. Silla did not unify Korea—it controlled somewhat more than half the peninsula, all of what is now South Korea, and small portions of what is North Korea. This included most of the rich rice-growing lands and a majority of the population, but most of the northern part of Korea was ruled by another state: Parhae, founded in 713. Koreans have long debated whether Parhae was a Korean state and thus Korea at this time was divided into north and south, or whether it was non-Korean. It is not an easy question to answer since there was not yet a single Korean language or culture. Most evidence suggests that Parhae was primarily populated by peoples who were not directly ancestral to modern Koreans; and most of it was outside the boundaries of Korea today. Even if Parhae is excluded from the mainstream of Korean history, the fact remains that the state constructed by Silla broke apart for a generation at the end of the 9th century. Nor did Silla's successor Koryŏ control all of what is now Korea. Only in the early 15th century did a Korean state govern a territory that neatly corresponds to the two Koreas today.

Another problem with seeing Silla as creating a unified Korean state is that it is difficult to say how unified or how Korean Silla was. It is not clear, and it is in fact unlikely, that there was a common ethnic identity or linguistic unity during the Silla period. The creation of what became an ethnically and linguistically homogeneous society with shared cultural identity came about only after many centuries. The process was far from complete when Silla came to an end. Furthermore, the kings of Silla struggled to create a unified, centralized state and had only mixed success in doing so.

Late Silla did, however, display patterns of political and social organization that characterized later Korea. It was a rigidly hierarchical society with hereditary ranks, dominated by powerful aristocratic families. These families derived their wealth from the ownership of land and slaves. Beneath the aristocracy were commoners. Some commoners were free peasants, others were tenant farmers, and others craft persons. There was little social mobility and commoners were kept in their place, not only by being excluded from positions in government, but by requirements that their clothes, homes, and carts should be different from those of the aristocracy. Below the commoners were slaves, and outcast groups who inherited lowly occupations such as butchers, tanners, and ferrymen. The nature of elite status evolved, but the basic social structure remained fundamentally unchanged to the end of the 19th century.

The monarch sat at the apex of society, but in reality he had to share power with the upper aristocracy known as the 'true bone'. In earlier times, the royal family belonged to a hereditary rank known as the 'sacred bone', a name that implied some religious or priestly authority. Kings claimed to be descended from ancestors who had supernatural origins. In the 7th century the sacred-bone line died out and kings were chosen from the true-bone rank aristocracy, thus losing some of their awe-inspiring quality. Leading families met in a council, the Hwabaek, an institution that rivalled the authority of the king; and they possessed their own private armies. The Hwabaek institution did not survive Silla, and eventually private armies disappeared, but mixed monarchical and aristocratic governance continued throughout the dynastic period.

No longer in its expansionary phase and facing common threats from Parhae, Tang Dynasty China welcomed Silla into its tributary system. Under this system, the court in the Silla capital Kyŏngju flattered the Chinese emperor's pretensions of being the ruler of all civilization, sending groups of emissaries with gifts to him.

Under the guise of an exchange of gifts or 'tribute' they would engage in trade while the emperor would bestow legitimacy upon the Korean kings. Through these missions a continual flow of Chinese art, literature, and technology entered the kingdom. Its officials wore Tang-style robes and its administration adopted Chinese nomenclature. Some members of the elite wrote poems and essays in classical Chinese. The court sponsored an academy that taught Chinese classics. Hundreds of Koreans, mostly members of the lower-ranked aristocracy, are known to have studied in China.

Silla, however, maintained both its political and cultural autonomy. In addition to the use of Chinese the elite wrote in Korean using Chinese characters mostly for their phonetic value, and the kingdom's administrative structure differed in many ways from that of Tang. More fundamentally, while the Tang state gradually reduced the power of the hereditary aristocracy, Silla's powerful aristocratic families never loosened their monopoly over important government posts. Korean kings were never able to concentrate control into their hands as effectively as Chinese emperors often succeeded in doing. And while anti-Buddhist sentiment asserted itself in late Tang, Buddhism's central place in Silla society and its links with the state remained undiminished (Figure 2).

In the 9th century Silla went into decline, linked in ways that are not fully understood with the political and economic decline of China at that time. Power gravitated to local strongmen, banditry plagued the countryside; tax revenues shrank, further weakening the state. In 900, a rebel in the south-west established a new Paekche state, and the next year another rebel proclaimed a new Koguryŏ state in the north. Historians have labelled these breakaway states Later Paekche and Later Koguryŏ. In 918, Later Koguryŏ's founder was assassinated by one of his commanders Wang Kŏn. He renamed it Koryŏ, a shortened form of Koguryŏ.

2. Pulguksa Temple in the Silla capital Kyŏngju.

Once more there was a struggle for supremacy among three kingdoms. This time it lasted three decades instead of three centuries. It is not clear if the fragmentation of Silla meant that the unification of 676 was in fact incomplete and the old regional loyalties and identities were reasserting themselves, or if Later Paekche and Later Koguryŏ were just names adopted by their founders to give a historical weight to their new states. Whatever the case, Wang Kŏn ended up the victor, putting together a reunified state under Koryŏ. His dynasty ruled Korea for more than four and a half centuries. Korea never again experienced political fragmentation.

Koryŏ

The state reassembled by Wang Kŏn in 935 remained mostly intact for 1,000 years. This statement needs qualification—there was a change in dynasties and a name change in 1392, but it remained essentially the same state although there were significant differences in thought, culture, and systems of government. Within its framework Korea went a long way toward

16

developing into an integrated society with a shared culture. Koryŏ (also spelled Goryeo), in fact, along with Chosŏn and Han'guk is one of the common names used today by Koreans for their country; the English word Korea is derived from it.

Wang Kŏn regarded his kingdom as a successor to both Koguryŏ and Silla. This is reflected in his new capital at Kaegyŏng (modern Kaesong) 50 km north of modern Seoul and just inside North Korea. It was near the centre of the peninsula between the former Silla capital Kyŏngju and the former Koguryŏ capital of Pyongyang, both of which Wang made his secondary capitals. To strengthen his link with Silla, Wang Kŏn married into the royal Kim family and appointed Silla aristocrats to key positions in his government. Later in the dynasty scholars emphasized Koryŏ links with Silla rather than with Koguryŏ. They were careful to point out that the last king of Silla had designated him as successor.

This was the position taken by historian Kim Pusik, himself a descendant of an old Sillan aristocratic lineage, in the *Samguk sagi* (History of the Three Kingdoms) completed in 1145. This traces the story of Korea from the mythical origins of the Three Kingdoms to the end of Silla in 935. It remains our most important source for ancient Korea. The *Samguk sagi* treats Silla as the unifier of the Three Kingdoms, leaving Parhae out of Korean history, and the Wang dynasty as the legitimate successor to the royal Silla Kim line. Before completing his work, Kim helped put down a revolt led by the monk Myo Ch'ŏng to transfer the capital to Pyongyang. So Kim Pusik not only kept the kingdom from shifting its centre to the north, he contributed to keeping Korean history anchored in the southern-based Silla state.

Wang Kŏn and his successors faced the same problem that the Silla kings did: how to create a centralized state out of a land of powerful warrior-aristocratic clans rooted in their home bases. Much of the countryside was controlled by these aristocratic families, who possessed their own private armies. The mountainous geography with many little valleys and ridges reinforced the autonomy of these regional strongmen, sometimes referred to as 'castle lords'. In an effort to bind them to his new dynasty Wang Kŏn married their daughters, twenty-eight altogether. But this only complicated the succession when upon his death the castle lords tried to put their sons-in-law on the throne.

King Kwangjong (r. 949–75), Wang Kŏn's fourth son, who came to the throne after a brief power struggle, tried to weaken the aristocracy by limiting the number of slaves they could own, providing land for their tenant farmers, and carrying out bloody purges of high-ranking officials from prominent families. These efforts were unsuccessful. He attempted to enhance his power and prestige by declaring himself to be *hwangje* (emperor), using the title previous reserved for the Chinese emperor. Although at this time China was divided, with a number of regional rulers claiming the title, it was nonetheless a break with tradition. He renamed Kaegyŏng as Hwangdo, meaning Imperial Capital. This challenged the principle held by educated Koreans that there was only one emperor, the ruler of China, and Kwangjong's successors abandoned imperial pretensions, resuming the humbler title of king. Only in 1897, near the end of the dynastic period, did a Korean king again call himself emperor. Efforts by the Koryŏ kings to create a centralized state remained limited. Most top positions in the kingdom's counties and prefectures were held by descendants of castle lords.

Kwangjong, however, carried out one measure that was effective in strengthening the state and attaching the aristocracy to it. He adopted the Chinese civil examination system to select officials for the state. In 958, seven men were selected to serve the kingdom after passing exams testing their mastery of Chinese classics, literary skills, and knowledge of geomancy. It was a modest start to what would evolve into the central institution for recruiting officials.

Gradually the civil service exams became the most important vehicle for entering high office. Those that passed them not only gained access to government office but acquired great prestige for themselves and their families. As a result more and more young aristocratic boys studied for them. The civil service exams over time transformed the Korean aristocracy from warriors into scholars and bureaucrats who loyally served the state. Preparation for the examinations acted as a means of homogenizing the elite as well as binding it to the state. Aspiring young aristocratic men studied the same curricula, sometimes together at a number of private schools that were created for this purpose. They also became knitted together in country-wide teacher–students networks and classmate bonds. A unified, shared culture among the aristocracy emerged, along with a strong identification with the kingdom they served. At the same time the state benefited from being governed by an increasingly literate bureaucracy.

The study of Chinese texts included those associated with Confucianism, a tradition developed in China which taught that the universe was a moral order and that all humans are connected with it and with each other in a web of relationships. Each individual had the moral duty and responsibility to adhere to the role appropriate to that relationship, whether it was being a parent or a child, a ruler or a subject. It viewed the world as a hierarchical order in which everyone was assigned a place. Confucianism, by emphasizing loyalty, authority, and hierarchy, provided a social and political philosophy that was appealing to Koryŏ rulers and the aristocratic elite. Confucian texts were taught in Late Silla's Academy, but during Koryŏ the philosophy became of greater importance and influence.

The officials who served the state were divided into *munban*, the civil officials, and the *muban*, those that served in the military. Together they made up the *yangban* or 'two sides' referring to the two sides that sat by the king. The aristocracy became so associated with serving the state that the term 'yangban' became synonymous with them. Aristocratic families were divided into lineages who studied for the civil exams and lineages who studied for the military exams. It is indicative of how much the nature of the elite was changing in Korea that the military lineages that upheld the old martial traditions became lower in social status than those from which the civil officials came.

While the yangban elite increasingly identified with and served the state, their refined, Chinese-style and Confucian-influenced culture reinforced the gap between them and commoners. The emphasis on bloodlines made that gap nearly insurmountable for an ambitious person of humble background. However, Koreans of all classes shared the Buddhist faith. Under aristocratic and royal patronage, monasteries grew rich, becoming major owners of lands and slaves. Originally Buddhism was the religion of the aristocracy, who favoured the Flower Garland (Hwaŏm) sect with its esoteric teachings and elaborate rituals. Buddhism took greater hold among the common people with the introduction of the Pure Land sect. Pure Land Buddhism focused on devotion to Amitabha, the *bodhisattva* or saint of mercy. It was a form of Buddhism accessible and appealing to the humble. No costly ceremonies or time-consuming rituals or mastery of sacred texts were needed to achieve the blessed afterlife, just prayers and devotion. Koryŏ continued the Silla practice, sponsoring the construction of temples.

The transformation of Koryŏ's aristocracy from a warrior to a Confucian-influenced service nobility was similar to the change the Chinese aristocracy had undergone with the implementation of the civil examinations a couple of centuries earlier. Yet many elements of Korean society did not change. The civil examinations in Korea differed from those in China by being more restrictive, allowing only those from noble lineages to take them. Unlike in China, where civil exams weakened the old aristocratic families, in Korea the elite families continued to maintain their dominance over society. Nor did they entirely lose their martial skills; horse riding and archery were still popular. Even monks maintained a warrior tradition and were ready to fight for the state.

In another contrast with China, the two sexes mixed freely. Men and women drank, danced, played cards, rode horses, and even participated in mixed gender polo games. A 12th-century Chinese visitor, Xu Jing, who left an account of Korean life, was shocked by the failure of Korean men to restrict the activities of their women. Women could divorce their husbands and gain custody of their children, and could inherit property—in fact, family property was divided equally among sons and daughters. A woman's property was hers even in marriage and she could pass it on to her children; women sometimes headed households. Korean women were, along with Japanese women at the time, among the least restricted in the civilized world.

Koryŏ's progress in creating an integrated state was reinforced by its need for a strong central military to deal with the northern barbarians. Mainly based in Manchuria, the northern tribal people maintained a way of life that Korea's elite once maintained. Unlike earlier Manchurian invaders, who entered the lush agricultural lands of the peninsula inhabited by small tribal societies and became their masters, these mounted warrior folk encountered a formidable state. After unsuccessfully resisting them, Koryŏ was forced to pay tribute to the Khitans and their state of Liao. Liao fell to another Manchurian group, the Jurchens, who conquered most of northern China where they founded the state of Jin in 1234. Koryŏ paid tribute to Jin and was spared a major invasion.

Not only did the Khitans and the Jurchens impose a heavy financial burden on Koryŏ, they also hindered Korean contact with China. The suspicious Chinese were reluctant to enter into sea-based trade and exchange with Koryŏ since it had established tributary relations with these Manchurian-based warrior-states. This was unfortunate for Koreans because this was the era of the prosperous Song dynasty, a high-water mark in China's pre-modern technological and economic development. Only in the late 11th and early 12th century when the power of Khitan was waning was Koryŏ fully able to trade with Song and benefit from its rich culture.

Military rule and the Mongol period

Koryŏ underwent a period of rule by the military lineages of the aristocracy. By the 12th century the *munban* lineages dominated the state while the *muban* military officials suffered a decline in status and were largely excluded from decision making. Even at times of crisis military command was given to civil officials. In 1170, this trend of civil domination was suddenly reversed when military officials seized power in a bloody coup led by Chŏng Chungbu, a commander of the royal guard. Chŏng and his military allies waited until King Ŭijong and his entourage were away on a visit to the temple, and then murdered much of his remaining court. They then seized the king and sent him to the remote Kŏje Island. Ŭijong was later rolled up in a blanket and drowned, a way to avoid shedding royal blood. Chŏng placed a puppet king on the throne, purged a number of civil officials, and created a Supreme Military Council staffed with *muban* to govern the kingdom. Many civil officials were allowed to maintain their positions, but the centre of power shifted to the military rulers, their retainers, and their slaves.

When the military seized power, they unleashed a generation of political and social instability. Generals fought each other for power in the capital, while peasant and slave revolts took place in the countryside. The turmoil finally came to an end in 1196 when General Ch'oe Chunghŏn seized power. Ch'oe restored order to Korea, putting down peasant revolts and slave rebellions, and restructuring the military to make it subordinate to him. His most radical move was to establish a dual government. He retained the king, the court officials, and the civil bureaucracy, much as it had been before the military coup. Alongside these institutions he created a parallel 'house government' staffed by his personal retainers and close allies. Real power was in this 'house government' directly under his control. So effectively did he maintain control over the country that he smoothly transferred power to his son Ch'oe U who further elaborated on the house government. Ch'oe U was succeeded by his son Ch'oe Hang.

Ch'oe Chunghŏn's dual government was, in many ways, similar to the system created by his Japanese contemporary Minamoto Yoritomo. In both Korea and Japan effective power passed from the court-centred aristocracy to the military in the late 12th century. In both, after a period of conflict, a strong effective ruler created a parallel military clan government that held real power while maintaining the monarch and older civil institutions. Yoritomo assumed the title of shogun or paramount military leader in 1192, just four years before Ch'oe established a similar military-led house government in Korea. Both Ch'oe and Yoritomo made use of an elaborate system of military retainers and military leaders who pledged their personal loyalty to them. Both patronized meditative Buddhism (*Sŏn* in Korean, *Zen* in Japanese) which rose in prominence in the two countries. The two systems of military-led dual governments were not entirely the same. The families that created Japanese warrior-government came from the provincial nobility, while the military rulers of Korea were more linked to the central aristocracy. Ch'oe Chunghŏn came from a distinguished line that traced itself to famed Silla scholar and official Ch'oe Ch'iwŏn. Korea continued to use the civil service exam to recruit officials, a practice not carried out in Japan. Still the parallels are striking. It is not clear, however, if and to what extent the developments in Korea and Japan at this time were connected.

Another difference between Japan and Korea was that the Ch'oe 'shogunate' continued for only three generations and then came to an end under the impact of the Mongols. The Koreans first encountered the Mongols in 1218. That year the forces of Genghis

23

Khan arrived at the border demanding that the Koreans pay tribute. This was to be in the form of clothes, furs, and horses. The last was particularly burdensome since Korea had little grazing land to raise the needed horses. When the Korean government stopped paying tribute the Mongols sent an invading army. Faced with this mighty force Koryŏ agreed to start paying tribute. To make sure that they did, the Mongols sent overseers to supervise the collection. The following year, the Mongol overseers were murdered and Ch'oe U stopped sending tribute again; the Mongols predictably returned with an even greater force under one of their commanders, Sartaq.

Rather than submitting to the Mongols, the Koryŏ court transferred to the island of Kanghwa north of modern Inchon (Inch'ŏn). A new capital with palaces, offices, and temples was built on this tiny 10– × 17-mile island just off the coast. From this bastion the Koreans waged a war of resistance for the next twenty-six years. After several failed attempts to force Koryŏ into submission the Mongols sent small forces to lay waste to the country. The result was catastrophic, with villagers massacred, homes destroyed, fields burned, and many captives taken away as slaves. After four years of this, the last Ch'oe ruler was killed in a coup, and a new government agreed to truce terms.

Korea was attached to the great Mongol empire, the largest contiguous land empire in history stretching from western Russia and Iran to Manchuria and Vietnam. Northern Koryŏ became a military zone that reported to the Mongol court, and the rest of the kingdom was under the authority of the Koryŏ kings, who ruled with the approval of the Great Khan. Since after 1279 the Mongols governed China as the Yuan dynasty, this bore resemblance to the traditional tributary system. The Mongol rulers of China, however, interfered more directly in Korean affairs, posting officials in Kaegyŏng. Mongol tribute demands were not ceremonial but could be burdensome. Especially burdensome was Korean support for the two Mongol invasions of Japan in 1274 and 1281. On orders

24

from the Mongols, Koreans supplied the ships and sailors for these two massive invasions. Both ended in failure when typhoons (referred to by the Japanese as the *kamikaze* or 'divine winds') arrived forcing the invaders to withdraw. Another difference was that, unlike its past relations with China, the Wang dynasty monarchs were required to marry Yuan princesses and so Koryŏ during this period is often called the 'son-in-law' state.

Koreans found themselves with compromised sovereignty, but for many it was a period of opportunity. Thousands served in the vast Mongol bureaucracy. Tens of thousands lived and worked in the Yuan capital Daidu (today's Beijing) and other parts of the cosmopolitan empire, mainly in China and southern Manchuria. They encountered people of diverse ethnic and religious groups and became exposed to new ideas and technologies. The latter included the production of cotton and gunpowder. It was at this time that Korean scholars became fully aware of Song Confucianism, known to Westerners as Neo-Confucianism (see Chapter 2).

By the mid-14th century the Yuan state weakened. In 1356, Zhu Yuanzhang, a former monk, established the Ming dynasty in Nanjing and drove the Mongols out of southern China. In 1368, Ming forces captured Beijing and the Mongols were forced back to their homeland where the remnant of their empire, now called the Northern Yuan, still controlled parts of Manchuria. Koryŏ abolished the Mongol offices in its capital and reasserted its full autonomy. But Koreans remained divided between pro-Mongol and pro-Ming factions. A pro-Ming general, Yi Sŏnggye, seized power in 1388. Four years later he made himself first monarch of the new Yi dynasty and renamed the kingdom Chosŏn.

The Mongol invasions and conquests both contributed to a Korean cultural and ethnic identity and made the society more cosmopolitan. During the years of resistance, the legend of Tan'gun was first recorded as the start of Korean history by the monk Iryŏn in his *Samguk yusa* (Record of the Three Kingdoms) and in the epic poem *Chewang un'gi* (Song of Emperors and Kings). Korean monks compiled the extant version of what is known as the *Tripitaka Koreana*, a vast collection of 80,000 woodblocks containing the most complete collection of Buddhist sutras anywhere. At the same time the Mongols made Korea, for the first time in its history, a full participant in a great multi-ethnic empire. When the Korean state regained full sovereignty, its people inherited a sense of collective identity strengthened by their resistance to the Mongols as well as the exposure to new ideas from their experience of being part of a larger Eurasian world.

Chapter 2
A Confucian society

For five centuries from 1392 to the arrival of modern imperialism in the late 1800s Korea underwent a continual process of cultural change and integration under the Chosŏn state and its Yi ruling family. The state's territorial boundaries stabilized to where they are today, its population became ethnically homogeneous, and their culture became profoundly Confucian. The process by which the inhabitants of the peninsula developed into a single people with a shared culture and identity, one clearly recognizable today as 'Korean', had begun long before. Under Chosŏn it was largely completed.

The establishment of the Chosŏn state by Yi Sŏnggye in 1392 did not mark a sharp change in the direction of Korean history. It was rather the same old Koryŏ kingdom under a new dynasty with a new capital Hanyang (today's Seoul) 30 miles (50 km) south of the old one, Kaesong. For the most part, the new dynasty was ruled by the same families and officials that had served in Koryŏ joined by men of military background like Yi and by some scholars from lesser aristocratic lineages. Yi Sŏnggye and his son T'aejong (r. 1400–18) pursued the same policies as had the early kings of Koryŏ—abolishing private armies, reforming the tax system, and strengthening monarchical power. There were some institutional changes. T'aejong was able to exert more direct central control over the countryside through the use of powerful royal governors to administer the eight provinces. Furthermore, unlike his Koryŏ predecessor, he was able to place centrally appointed magistrates to head all the counties and prefectures. Most significantly, Korea under the five centuries of Chosŏn changed as generations of reformers carried out efforts to bring the political and social order in line with Confucian principles. Gradually, through their persistent efforts, Confucian-based cultural norms pervaded every social class giving a greater uniformity and unity to Korean society.

Creating a Confucian state

Under the Chosŏn dynasty Neo-Confucianism became the state ideology. What was once a Buddhist-Confucianist state became a Neo-Confucianist one. Confucianism, a system of ethical, social, and political thought, was not new to Korea. It had been part of the mix of Chinese learning that had been entering the peninsula since the Three Kingdoms period. Confucian teachings became part of the curricula for the civil exams in Koryŏ. During the Mongol period, however, Korean scholars became aware of a new reinterpretation of Confucianism that had flowered in China during the 11th and 12th centuries. Koreans called it by varying names, including 'study of the Way [of Heaven]', but today modern scholars refer to it as Neo-Confucianism. Thinkers in the Neo-Confucian tradition aimed at removing what they regarded as the superstitious Buddhist, Daoist, and other corruptions to the line of teachings associated with Confucius and his followers. While in reality Neo-Confucianism was a reinterpretation of Confucianism that made it a more all-embracing belief system with many aspects of a religion, its adherents believed they were recapturing and reviving the ancient wisdom of Confucius and the sages before him.

Korean advocates of Neo-Confucianism were especially dogmatic, intolerant of divergent views and insistent on the need to remodel society based on its principles. They sought nothing less than to create a great virtuous and harmonious society in accordance with the Way of Heaven. Most of the core principles emphasized by these Neo-Confucianist reformers—loyalty, hierarchy, respect for tradition, the importance of family, and the need for all members of society to adhere to the roles assigned to them by the laws of nature—were not new. But their intolerance of other beliefs was a break with the Korean tradition of accepting multiple forms of spirituality. Buddhism, shamanism, nature worship, elements of Daoism, as well as Confucianism, had coexisted and borrowed from each other. Individual Koreans might follow them all. The reformers, however, were staunchly opposed to Buddhism which they saw as self-centred, focusing on oneself and not one's duty to society; and they regarded monks as parasitical, contributing nothing to society. At their insistence, the state closed temples in the capital and banned monks from public affairs. Most temples were stripped of their slaves and landholdings. Under the relentless attacks by Neo-Confucianists and the state they increasingly dominated, Buddhism retreated into the margins of Korean society. Although still widely practised, it was no longer at the centre of public life.

The Neo-Confucianists placed a great deal of importance on the role of government in creating a virtuous society. For them the new dynasty was an opportunity to reform government in order to reform society. Neo-Confucianist scholars such as Chŏng Tojŏn were among the most ardent supporters of the Chosŏn dynasty and an important part of the coalition that brought Yi Sŏnggye to power. The reformers then worked to see to it that the monarch, his court, and his public servants carried out their roles in accordance with the Way. They pursued their project of bringing the state in line with Confucian principles less by radical institutional change than by reforming the inherited organs of the state.

An important vehicle for their project was a set of three institutions known as the Censorate. Borrowed originally from China, the Censorate consisted of boards of scholars who examined the backgrounds of potential appointees to state office and their families. Candidates for office not only needed records of unblemished moral character but had to come from families which were free from scandal. Even a wayward grandparent could be grounds for disqualification. They also reviewed the conduct of officials while in office to see that they were acting properly, not just in their public but also in their private life. Another of the Censorate's major functions was to monitor the conduct of the king. Censors frequently admonished monarchs for unethical or otherwise improper behaviour. In short, they were the moral guardians or moral police of the state. Since censors were well schooled in the tenets of Neo-Confucianism and firm adherents of them, the Censorate acted as one of the institutional bases for the great undertaking of making Korea a truly Confucian society.

The reformers placed importance on the ruler as the upholder of the moral and social order of society. He did this through his personal example of virtuous conduct and by governing with a concern for the welfare of his subjects. They insisted that the king attend daily lectures by scholars to remind him of his moral duties, and that his words and conversations with officials be recorded by historians for posterity. Compiling history was an important project since it could be used to educate future rulers. Another instrument for promoting a virtuous government was through the civil service exams. These were especially important, not only to see that men of merit served in government, but since their content was based on the study of canonical texts they were a major means of indoctrinating the elite into Confucian principles.

Creating a virtuous government that reflected the Way of Heaven proved a long-term project. Fifteenth-century officials, even monarchs, continued to consult Buddhist monks and shamans; and kings often failed to attend the daily lectures. Yet, over time the state and the ruling class adopted most elements of the official interpretation of Confucianism promulgated by Neo-Confucian reformers. Deviation from this was ruled heterodoxy and dangerous.

Although the 16th century produced some first-rate Confucian thinkers such as Yi Hwang (better known as T'oegye) and Yi I (better known as Yulgok), in general Korean intellectual life was dominated by a dogmatic rigidness not found in contemporary China or Japan.

As the state became more Confucian, the upper class became more linked to it. Even more than was the case in Koryŏ, serving the state became the principal means of confirming and enhancing status, of protecting wealth and acquiring power and influence. The main way to gain office was through the state examinations. Each of the country's 300 counties had a state-sponsored school to prepare young men for the exams and educate them in the principles of the Way. These were supplemented by hundreds of private academies. The law of avoidance meant that if a young man passed the exams and gained an official post, he was not allowed to serve in the home area. Thus, the near universal focus on the exams, the common curricula, the circulation of the officials around the kingdom, and the networks of school ties acted as a process of homogenizing the yangban. This process of creating a like-minded, state-centred elite was reinforced by the fact that almost all spent some time in Seoul.

One way, however, that Chosŏn Korea deviated from Neo-Confucianism was the importance of hereditary status. This was a contradiction with the Confucian belief in government by merit. But efforts by some reformers to open public office to those of humble status were not successful. Rather the Chosŏn state was the enforcer of social ranks. Neo-Confucian literati were concerned that everyone should know their rank so that order could be maintained—so much so that they developed the *hop'ae* system in which people wore identity tags indicating their status. Yangban wore yellow poplar tags, commoners small wooden ones, and there were big wooden ones for slaves. Yangban serving as high-ranking officials wore ivory identity tags, lower-ranked officials ones of deer horn.

Creating a Confucian society

Korean Confucianism was distinguished from that of its neighbours not by doctrine but by its careful and often rigid adherence to the rituals, and by the persistent efforts of reform-minded scholars and officials to make most social institutions adhere to its principles. Reformers placed special emphasis on the family and on making sure that each person correctly performed his or her role in the family. Rituals and ceremonies reinforced these roles. These were to be carried out in accordance with canonical texts such as *Family Rituals* by the 12th-century Chinese scholar Zhu Xi. Older Korean customs such as those associated with marriage were altered to conform to the rituals and practices laid out by these texts. Another concern of Neo-Confucianists was that everyone carry out his or her duty to marry in order to perpetuate the family line. This become so important that young people who died before marriage were often married posthumously to another boy or girl who also died prematurely.

The centre of Korean ritual life became the rites to family ancestors or *chesa*. This not only emphasized the importance of family lineage but also the fundamental principle of filial piety (*hyo*). Filial piety, the respect and loyalty to one's parents, was the basis for all loyalty and duty which were virtues necessary to maintain a stable, harmonious society. To reinforce respect for and loyalty to not only one's parents but all one's direct ancestors the state mandated that all perform the *chesa*. It also required three years of mourning when a parent died; their death date was commemorated annually thereafter by a special ceremony.

Neo-Confucianist reforms greatly impacted the relationships between men and women. Women had to be subservient and obedient to men, and the distinction between men and women had to be strictly maintained. In the 15th century laws were passed prohibiting women from riding horses, playing polo,

Korea

32

or engaging in activities that were part of the male sphere. Women lost the right to divorce their husbands and to gain custody of their children. They no longer shared inheritance equally with their male siblings, could no longer keep their property in marriage, and could not mix freely with men. Women had to be chaste and loyal to their in-laws. Widows were no longer allowed to remarry since they were to be loyal to their husbands for eternity. Girls were often married in childhood. If their husbands died early, even before they were fully grown adults, which was not uncommon in pre-modern times since death rates were high, they were still prohibited from remarrying. Women were held to a high standard of chastity. Any questioning of a woman's virtue could bring dishonour to her entire family. Young girls were sometimes given a *p'aedo*, a small knife to commit suicide with should that happen.

The spheres of the two genders were kept so separate that houses often had different entrances—one for men and one for women. Inside the home there were men's and women's quarters separated by the kitchen. Late in Chosŏn, concern for keeping men and women apart went even further. In Seoul, to make sure that they did not mix in public there were certain hours of the day marked by ringing a bell when only women could be on the street. At all other times, only men could move about. Many upper-class women lived secluded lives behind high walls with little exposure to men other than relatives. Even male physicians could treat female patients only from behind a screen, using the vibrations of a string to feel their pulse. Elite Korean women went from living among the least to among the most socially restricted lives in Asia. There were some exceptions such as *kisaeng*, female entertainers who played a role in society similar to Japanese geisha, and *mudang*, female shamans; but both were of low social status (Figure 3).

Strict adherence to Confucian norms of behaviour helped to distinguish the yangban elite from the commoners who did not

3. Korean yangban with *kisaeng*, 18th century.

have the luxury of adhering to all its rules. Men and women had to work together in the field at planting, harvesting, and other busy times, and commoners could not afford all the proper rituals or the three years of mourning. Yangban men with their white clothes, derived from these long periods of mourning dress, and with their black horsehair hats were clearly differentiated from commoners. Mastering the Confucian classics and adhering to the correct rituals helped define being members of the elite, since others did not have the time and luxury to do so.

Most Koreans were peasants living humble lives. Many owned land, but often too little to support a family so that they also worked lands owned by the elite. They lived in their own sections of villages and towns separate from the aristocracy and were excluded from public life. Between the commoners and the yangban was a small hereditary in-between class consisting of clerks who staffed the local government offices and skilled specialists who took special exams to become physicians, geomancers, and interpreters. At the bottom of society were the outcaste groups such as butchers and tanners, and slaves. Slavery was far more common in Korea than in its East Asian neighbours. Both aristocrats and the state owned slaves. In early Chosŏn perhaps one-third of the population were slaves. However, in the 18th and 19th centuries the institution declined. State-owned slavery was abolished in 1801 but some private slaves still existed until the 1890s.

Yet, despite the rigid gaps between yangban and the other social classes, Confucian customs and values were absorbed by the non-elite groups. Yangban gave regular sermons to villagers on Confucian principles, and many commoners sent their sons to village schools, *sŏdang*, where they were taught basic literacy by reading Confucian works. Ordinary people began offering rites to the ancestors and adopting the terminology of filial piety and distinction between the sexes. A widely shared respect for learning contributed to rising male literacy rates among commoners, although the civil exams were effectively closed to them. By the 18th century, if not earlier, pervasive use of the language of Confucianism and a devotion to its rituals was characteristic of Koreans of all social classes.

Its greater adherence to an orthodox version of Confucianism may have contributed to another way Korea differed from its East Asian neighbours—its lack of commercial development. Compared to China or Japan, the country was less urbanized, the merchant class smaller and less wealthy, and the volume of trade was more modest. Geography is one explanation for this. China, like Europe, had great rivers that facilitated transport; Japan had navigable coastal waters linking population centres, most significantly the Inland Sea. Korea had neither. The mountains and hills made overland travel difficult, the rivers did not connect regions of the country, and then there were the high tides and sandbars that made coastal navigation challenging. As a result, trade was often over narrow mountain footpaths where pedlars carrying A-frame backpacks were their own beasts of burden.

But geography can be overcome, and Koreans were able to construct a fairly centralized and uniform government in spite of living in a country of valleys and little plains separated by mountains. Other factors that contributed to this modest level of commercial activity included the policy of the Chosŏn state to discourage the mining of precious metals lest it attract the attention of China. This hindered the production of coins. Instead, transactions were often conducted in bolts of cotton or other cumbersome mediums of exchange. The most common explanation given for Korea's lack of a vigorous commercial sector, however, is the Confucian disdain for commerce, especially among the dominant yangban class. Yet there were signs that attitudes were changing in late Chosŏn; a number of scholars called for the need to develop commerce and the government began to increase the use of money transactions and ended restrictive merchant licensing practices.

Chosŏn's Confucianization can be exaggerated. Buddhism receded but did not disappear. The mountain monasteries continued to provide a safe retreat from the stresses of life; and Buddhist priests were often called upon to preside at funerals. Confucianism acknowledged no gods, afterlife, or eternal soul. Nonetheless, most Koreans lived a world inhabited by *kwisin* (spirits). There were spirits of the dead that could haunt them, bring disease and misfortune, and required a shaman to placate them. Even yangban and kings sometimes called upon shamans to deal with them. Spirits lived in trees, rocks, and striking geological features. Almost every temple had a shrine to Sanshin the mountain spirit. Household gods such as those of the kitchen, the gate, and those dwelling in storage jars were given offerings by women in household rituals. Each village had a shrine for the local guardian god. Buildings and gravesites were situated according to *p'ungsu* (geomancy), the belief that certain configurations of land were auspicious or had spiritual power. Seoul itself was laid out with North Mountain protecting the city from malevolent forces from the north and the Han River safeguarding it from the south. Yet spirit worship remained a mostly private affair and never matched Confucianism for importance. Only Confucianism served as an ideological basis for government, ethics, and social norms.

The zealousness with which Koreans adopted Neo-Confucianism gave their culture a distinctive nature while the adoption of its beliefs and values by all social classes contributed to the uniformity of their society. To a greater degree than with their East Asian neighbours, the centrality of Confucianism was a core feature of Korean cultural identity. Many Confucian beliefs and values were challenged and openly denounced by Koreans in the late 19th and 20th centuries as Korea underwent a long, painful process of modernization. Yet the influence of Confucianism was still apparent in both North and South Korea in the 21st century.

Securing the borders, becoming a homogeneous society

Under the early Chosŏn kings Korea's borders became fixed to where they are today. These boundaries were established as part of the effort to secure their frontiers. To the south, early Chosŏn kings dealt with the threat from Japanese pirates known as *waegu*. In 1443, King Sejong (r. 1418–50) reached an agreement which allowed Japanese merchants to trade at authorized southern ports and the raids abated. To the north King Sejong had to deal with raids by Jurchens tribal folk based in Manchuria. In order to protect the country he pushed the border further north to the Yalu and Tumen Rivers. Except for minor adjustments made in 1712 after Manchuria had become incorporated into the Chinese Empire, this is still the boundary between North Korea and China. The Chosŏn state encouraged those Jurchens who lived within the new boundaries of Korea to marry Koreans and adopt Korean culture. This was not completely successful at first, and there were two rebellions by Jurchen minorities in the 15th century, but eventually the tribal peoples in these frontier areas were absorbed into Korean society. The state then settled much of the sparsely populated north with Korean families from the southern part of the country. These were mostly poor landless peasants, and people of slave or outcaste background who now had the opportunity of owning their own farms. Settling the north was a gradual process, especially difficult in the remote, rugged Hamgyŏng province in the north-east with a climate and topography that made agriculture precarious. Yet, eventually, because of this policy of assimilation and settlement, the area became integrated into the rest of Korea.

Since few Koreans ventured beyond the Yalu and Tumen the political boundaries of Korea became the ethnic-linguistic boundaries as well. By the 17th century the Korean language had evolved into modern Korean, the language spoken today. Regional dialects existed but they were mutually comprehensible, more so than was the case in many societies of similar size such as Italy or Vietnam. There were no known speakers of any other language in Korea, nor, with the assimilation of the Jurchens, any ethnic or tribal minorities. Few societies in the world were so ethnically and linguistically uniform.

At the same time, Korea became a more culturally uniform society. Symbolic of that culture was the creation of *Hangul*, the Korean alphabet, in the 15th century. Koreans mainly wrote in classical Chinese. When they wrote in Korean they did so with Chinese characters, developing several methods of doing so. The problem was that the two languages could hardly be more different. Under King Sejong a committee of scholars developed a phonetic alphabet that not only accommodated the complex Korean sound system but based the letters themselves on stylized shapes of the tongue and mouth when making a sound. The work was finished in 1443 and was promoted in 1446 with a manual

Hunmin Chŏngŭm ('correct sounds for instructing the people'). In modern times *Hangul* has become a symbol of national pride and uniqueness. However, the yangban class preferred to write in classical Chinese, labelling the Korean alphabet the 'vulgar script' or 'women's script', implying that it was only good for untutored females. It was only in the 20th century that it became the main form for writing Korean and a symbol of Korean identity and cultural achievement.

While the distinctive *Hangul* writing system did not come into universal use during the Chosŏn period, many other customs and traditions marked the cultural boundaries between Koreans and non-Koreans. All Koreans wore distinctive clothes derived from early China and Mongol era dress, quite different from the clothes worn by men and women in contemporary China or Japan. Koreans lived in homes with interior and exterior designs that set them apart from their East Asian neighbours. These homes were heated in the cold winters by the system called *ondol* in which floors were warmed. While much of Korean art, literature, and music was derived from China they gradually evolved into more uniquely Korean forms.

Chosŏn in East Asia

Korea's often troubled relationship with its neighbours contributed to a common sense of Korean identity. Korea could never escape the reality of being surrounded by bigger, more powerful, and potentially dangerous neighbours. Chosŏn's efforts to cope with the challenges from them strengthened popular attachment of Koreans to the state and helped nurture a sense of collective identity among them.

After the frontiers were secured in the 15th century Chosŏn's next great threat came in the late 16th century from Japan. In 1592, Hideyoshi Toyotomi, a warrior who became ruler of Japan, carried out a plan to subdue Korea. His aim was to use the peninsula as a base for conquering China. In what was the largest overseas invasion in history up to that time, a quarter of a million men began crossing the Korea Straits, landing in Pusan. Caught by surprise, the unprepared Koreans were quickly overrun by the well-trained Japanese forces equipped with muskets as well as swords and pikes. In just three weeks they were in Seoul. The fleeing court called on China for help. Ming China, alarmed by the prospect of a new threat near its north-eastern border, responded immediately. Chinese forces stopped the invaders at Pyongyang. Eventually the Japanese were forced to withdraw to the southern parts of Korea. From there they launched a renewed invasion in 1597 but this time the better-prepared Koreans along with their Chinese allies were able to contain the Japanese advance. In 1598, Hideyoshi died and the Japanese withdrew from the peninsula.

The invasion devastated Korea, and its memory has been used in modern times to inflame anti-Japanese sentiment, while China's intervention resulted in Chosŏn's gratitude and reverence for the Ming dynasty. The war also produced one of Korea's great heroes, Admiral Yi Sunsin (1545–98). Yi supervised the construction of a fleet of ships that carried on a successful naval campaign, sinking hundreds of Japanese vessels and disrupting the Japanese supply lines. One of Admiral Yi's innovations was the *kŏbuksŏn* 'turtle ship', believed by many to be the world's first iron-clad vessels, pre-dating the *Monitor* and the *Merrimack* in the US Civil War by more than two and a half centuries. These proved resistant to Japanese naval gunfire and were designed to ram and sink enemy ships. Admiral Yi Sunsin died in combat toward the end of the conflict, becoming one of Korea's most admired figures. Following the failure of the court to protect the people against the invaders, many ordinary Koreans organized their own resistance. Their efforts against a foreign invader may well have contributed to their common identity as a Korean people.

From the early 17th century to the late 19th century, Korea maintained peaceful relations with Japan, trading and occasionally sending a diplomatic mission to Edo (Tokyo). The Korean visitors to Japan found the society falling short of being fully civilized. Their knowledge of and adherence to Confucian principles were inadequate, the sexes mixed too freely, and they claimed to have an emperor when there could be only one emperor presiding under Heaven, the one in Beijing. Koreans maintained more tentative contact with other countries such as Vietnam as well as with Okinawa and some other South-East Asian lands. In general, the Koreans regarded these more distant neighbours as also more distant from adherence to the Way, which reinforced pride in their own achievements.

Chosŏn's most important relationship was with China. Koreans often identified their land by reference to its geographic position with its giant neighbour. This is clear from the names they called their country—Haedong ('East of the Sea'), or Taedong ('Great East') both referring to being east of China, or 'Chosŏn', which can be interpreted as meaning morning country—again loosely translated as 'east of China'. China was 'Chungguo' or 'Chunghwa' 'Middle Kingdom' or 'Central Civilization'. Korean maps showed China in the centre of the world; officials regarded the Chinese emperor as the only emperor, a ruler without a peer. His approval was important for Korean kings to legitimize themselves. That their kingdom was right next to China, and that their ambassadors in Beijing were often given a seat closest to the emperor on ceremonial occasions, was a source of pride and reassurance that they were near the centre of civilization. And China was the home of the ancient legendary sage emperors, of Confucius and Mencius, and of the highly revered Neo-Confucian thinker Zhu Xi.

Seeking the legitimacy that recognition from the Chinese emperor conferred, Korean kings sent regular tribute missions to Beijing.

Over time these increased from one every three years to three a year. Hundreds of officials and their staff went on them, providing opportunities for trade, and for keeping up with the intellectual, cultural, and fashion trends in the Middle Kingdom. Korean admiration for China was only reinforced by the gratitude they felt for the Ming dynasty's intervention that saved them from Hideyoshi's hordes.

But in the mid-17th century developments challenged the way Koreans thought about China. In the early 17th century a Jurchen group called the Manchus founded a new state in Manchuria and began the conquest of China. The Manchus twice invaded Korea in 1627 and 1636, forcing the Koreans into paying tribute to them and breaking off ties with the Ming. In 1644, the Manchus took control of Beijing and established the Qing dynasty. Under this new dynasty the Chosŏn court resumed its tributary relations with China, dutifully sending its tribute missions. However, the Koreans were uneasy with the Qing since they regarded the new dynasty as 'barbarian'. While outwardly carrying out their traditional role as a loyal tributary, the Korean court secretly maintained a shrine to the Ming. They dated documents according to the old Ming calendar not the new Qing, thereby symbolically retaining loyalty to the old dynasty and delegitimizing the new one.

The Chinese Empire had in practice always been a multi-ethnic one, and imperial dynasties were often at least partly of Inner Asian origin. Furthermore, the Qing were great patrons of Confucianism and much of Chinese culture, which flourished under their rule. Yet Koreans continued to see the ruling dynasty as semi-barbarian, and they looked down on the Chinese elite as those who had compromised their principles and their dignity by obeying the alien Manchus. Not all Koreans held the Qing Empire in disdain. In the 18th century some Chosŏn writers praised the commercial development in China. In general, however, after the mid-17th century Koreans saw China as a society that had deviated somewhat from the path of civilization by submitting to barbarian rule.

Late Chosŏn

From the late 17th century, the educated elite of Korea began to re-evaluate their society and its place in the civilized world. China was under the rule of barbarians, and the Japanese were never fully civilized, so that Koreans were now the truest adherents to the Way; their society was the last bastion of Confucian principles in their purest form. Koreans still held great deference toward China as the home of civilization, the elite still composed in Chinese, and their writings were filled with references to classical China. Scholars showed interest in new intellectual trends such as Evidential Learning of Qing China, which Korean envoys encountered on trips to China. These new ways of thinking are often referred to by modern scholars as 'Practical Learning'. But they now showed greater interest in their own land.

Scholars and artists in the 18th and early 19th centuries were increasingly focusing on their own society for inspiration. The literati wrote histories, compiled geographies, and drew maps of Korea. Artists such as Kim Hongdo depicted the everyday life of Koreans from all classes including farmers in the field, weavers, and people attending village markets or playing traditional sports. Other painters devoted themselves to capturing the scenic spots of the country, others to recording its beautiful women. There was also a blurring of non-elite and elite culture. Yangban continued to write poems and essays in classical Chinese, but they also read and often anonymously wrote popular novels. An example was *The Story of Ch'unghyang*, written in the 18th century and still well known among Koreans today. Both traditional genres of Chinese-style paintings and the local tradition of folk paintings, *minhwa*, flourished. A new type of performance, *p'ansori*, raised folk singing and storytelling to an art form, providing a unique Korean cultural expression which was appreciated by all social classes (Figure 4).

Korea in the 18th century was a politically stable and prosperous Confucian kingdom. Life at the court in the 16th to 18th centuries was characterized by fierce competition for high positions in the state by rival factions. These were based on personal ties of loyalty as well as ideological differences. Those that lost out in power

4. Chosŏn era *sŏdang* (village school), after Kim Hong-do, *Album of Scenes from Daily Life*, early 19th century.

struggles were exiled to remote parts of the kingdom or even in some cases executed. However, in the 18th century under two able kings, Yŏngjo (r. 1724–76) and Chŏngjo (r. 1776–1800), a period of relative political stability was achieved. It was a time of prosperity and a cultural flowering.

After a terrible famine in 1693 to 1695, the population rebounded and probably peaked in the late 1700s at around thirteen million. Modest but significant improvements in agriculture—the increased use of double cropping and fertilizer, the use of more efficient ploughs, and the introduction of new food crops such as the potato and the sweet potato—increased output so that it kept up with population growth. Careful forest management prevented the problem of deforestation and ensured a supply of wood for construction and for the charcoal used to heat homes in the cold winters. Commerce, while still modest, expanded. There was an increased use of money, and farmers were entering the market economy by growing cash crops such as cotton and tobacco, the latter introduced in the 17th century. Women too seemed to be increasingly contributing to household incomes by making textiles at home for sale. In general, there were signs that family incomes were rising, if only modestly.

In the early 19th century there were some signs of trouble. Court politics was dominated by rival families who took turns placing weak kings on the throne. There was a drop in agricultural productivity, possibly due to environmental degradation, and even a decline in population. There was a serious rebellion in 1812 in the northern part of the country fuelled by resentment over regional discrimination and anger at excessive taxation. A rice riot shook Seoul in 1833. In 1862, the so-called Chinju Rebellion fuelled by corruption and high taxes spread across parts of southern Korea. A disturbing new religion, Christianity, gained a very small but growing number of followers. Another new religion called Tonghak (Eastern Learning) emerged in the 1860s. It combined ideas from

Confucianism, Christianity, and folk beliefs and called for social reform. Yet none of these rose to the level where they posed a serious threat to the political and social order. It was only the intrusion of Western imperialism into East Asia in the mid-19th century that brought about a century of upheaval and gave birth to modern Korea.

Chapter 3
From kingdom to colony

In the late 19th and early 20th centuries Korea became exposed to the new Western-dominated world of modern imperialism. As a result, the political and social order was seriously challenged, and the very existence of the state was threatened. Koreans responded by carrying out reforms and rethinking their ideas about their society and its place in the world. Despite their efforts at meeting the challenges it faced, their country fell under direct foreign rule for the first time in its recorded history. These experiences were not unique to Koreans. For most of the people of Asia and Africa this period brought foreign, usually Western, domination and the disruption of the traditional patterns of life. However, with their limited connections to the world outside East Asia, Koreans were especially unprepared for the intrusion of modern imperialism.

Yet Korea had some strengths. It did not have ethnic or sectarian divides that characterized many other countries confronted by modern imperialism; elites and commoners, despite a large social gap, shared a common culture. It was ruled by a class of scholar-bureaucrats who had a strong sense of collective identity and attachment to a centralized state. Furthermore, Koreans had a long tradition of learning from other societies. These advantages were not enough to prevent Korea from becoming a Japanese colony. They do, however, help explain the speed with which some Koreans adjusted to the technological, institutional, and intellectual challenges of modernization, and the intense, passionate nationalism that emerged among the Korean people.

Korea's changing place in the world

Until the late 19th century Korea's contact with the wider world was limited. This was due to both the country's geographic distance from the world's major international exchange routes and the Chosŏn state's policy of restricting contact with foreigners. Korea had never been entirely open to outsiders, but after the trauma of the Japanese and Manchu invasions and the shock of China falling to barbarians late Chosŏn so sealed itself off from the outside world that 19th-century Westerners labelled it the 'Hermit Kingdom'. Chosŏn regulations prohibited Koreans from travelling abroad except on authorized embassies. Boats were restricted in size to prevent fishermen or merchants from sailing to another country. Foreigners were not permitted to enter the country, with two exceptions: the Japanese were allowed to trade at Pusan and Chinese missions came to Seoul. But the Japanese in Pusan were confined to a walled compound and the Chinese missions followed a prescribed route then entered the capital through a special gate into a walled compound. Unauthorized Koreans were prohibited from having contact with the visitors.

While these restrictions bring to mind comparisons with contemporary North Korea, Chosŏn's isolation can be overdrawn. Koreans showed a lively curiosity about their neighbours and wrote many published accounts of their travels to China and Japan. Nor were they completely unaware of the West. Korean visitors to Beijing met with the Jesuit mission there, and Korean scholars read and commented on Chinese translations of Western science, medicine, and geography. They were often impressed with European skills at mathematics and astronomy. European clocks were imported as novelties. Yet few Westerners made it to Korea and no Korean is known to have travelled to Europe and returned.

For most members of the elite, Europe was a distant society only on the periphery of their consciousness.

This began to change with the introduction of Christianity. In the late 18th century a handful of yangban converted after being exposed to Catholicism from their encounters with the Jesuit mission in Beijing. The Chosŏn king, worried that it would distract young scholars from their studies, ruled it a heresy in 1785. Soon after, when it became known that the pope had ruled that family rites and belief in Christianity were incompatible, becoming a Christian meant violating the basic ethical norms of Confucian society. A convert was executed in 1791 for failing to prepare a memorial tablet to his mother. In 1801, 300 converts were put to death. Alarm over the potential danger the new faith posed increased when one Korean Christian sent a letter to the pope requesting help in forcing the Korean king to allow religious freedom. In the 1830s, several French priests were smuggled into the country and their activities led to more executions in 1839. Despite this, the Christian community grew to perhaps 20,000 by the 1860s; many were yangban from out-of-power factions.

However, it was only in the mid-19th century that the West became a serious threat to Korea and its neighbours. Koreans watched while China suffered a humiliating defeat by the British in the Opium War, 1839–42. This was followed by the American opening of Japan to trade and diplomacy in 1854, a second European war with China that led to a brief Anglo-French occupation of Beijing in 1860, and Russia's annexation of Chinese territory that same year. The last gave Russia a short border with Korea. As these events were unfolding, Chosŏn officials rebuffed several attempts by British, French, and Russian ships to open trade, reasserting that the country was not interested in commerce or relations with distant lands. In 1864, Taewŏn'gun, the father and regent of a young King Kojong, responded to more illegal entries of French priests into the country by executing them along with several thousand Korean Catholics. France retaliated to the killing of their citizens by sending a force of seven ships and 600 men to Korea in October 1866 but met fierce resistance and accomplished little. That same year, a heavily armed American merchant vessel, the *General Sherman*, sailed up the Taedong River to Pyongyang in an attempt to inaugurate trade. After it was told to leave, a confused altercation took place in which the ship was burned and its crew were killed. Five years later, in 1871, the United States, having learned about the missing ship's fate, launched their own punitive expedition of five ships and 1,200 men that also attacked the fortifications on Kanghwa Island, killing hundreds of Korean defenders.

It was not Westerners but the Japanese who 'opened' Korea. In 1868, the shogunate was overthrown in a revolution labelled the 'Meiji Restoration'. The new government, carrying out a modernization programme, used newly acquired modern naval vessels to threaten Korea. In 1876, King Kojong, who had assumed power from his hardline father, rather than risk conflict with his neighbour across the Strait, conceded to Japanese demands to establish formal diplomatic relations with the new Meiji government and to open select ports to Japanese merchants. In 1882, Seoul established relations with the United States and sent a mission there too. All this marked a new chapter in Korean history.

Late Chosŏn efforts at reforms

Koreans both inside and outside the government were quick to grasp the need to learn from outside powers and make major changes to survive and flourish in the new world they were facing. However, they confronted several serious problems. Koreans were not only suddenly flooded with new ideas about government, society, science, technology, and international affairs all at once, they had to find ways of applying them to their society. At the same time, they had to choose between different models and conflicting advice on how to carry out reforms. And they had to deal with the efforts of powerful neighbours to conquer or control them.

Soon after its 'opening' in 1876 the court sent officials to China to study the reforms being carried out there. Koreans had long regarded China as a centre for culture and learning so that was a natural model to learn from. Many were impressed with the Chinese 'Self-Strengthening' programme of cautiously borrowing Western technology, especially military technology, and engaging in Western-style diplomacy while maintaining their basic political institutions and values. Korean fact-finding missions also went to Japan, which offered a more radical response to imperialism—a thorough adaptation of Western legal, political, and educational institutions while maintaining their imperial house as a symbol of the country's traditions. Some Koreans decided to learn directly from the West, primarily by going to the United States or learning from the American missionaries who were arriving in the country in the 1880s.

While searching for ways to navigate this new world, Koreans found themselves in the middle of three empires: the declining Chinese, the expanding Russian, and the rising Japanese. Each was seeking to gain some measure of control over Korea and was actively intervening in its affairs. China, struggling to keep its empire intact, sought to make Korea subordinate to Beijing and keep it out of the hands of another power. Russia, expanding in the Pacific region, looked at the peninsula to the south with an interest in its warm water ports and resources. The modernizing regime of Meiji Japan regarded control over Korea as a way of securing its periphery and providing a market for its goods.

The Chosŏn court in the early 1880s proceeded cautiously, creating some new institutions including a new body to conduct foreign relations patterned on those China had recently created. A group of young reformers who had been sent to Japan felt this was insufficient to deal with the crisis the country faced. Known as the Enlightenment Party they seized power in December 1884 with the intention of carrying out more sweeping governmental and social reforms on the model of the Meiji reformers in Japan.

The coup was short-lived. The Chinese, who had some troops stationed at their legation, intervened and the Enlightenment Party leaders were killed or fled the country.

The rash actions by more radical reformers and the Chinese intervention were a serious setback for Korea. This eliminated and discredited many of those who advocated a more accelerated pace of reform and empowered the Chinese, who exercised a considerable measure of control over Korea for the next decade. The Chinese stifled Korean efforts at reforms that might diminish Beijing's influence over it. They made it difficult for Koreans to travel abroad, pressured the Chosŏn government to order students abroad to return home, and blocked efforts by Seoul to open embassies in Western countries. But the Chinese could not keep out foreign missionaries who opened schools and hospitals and exposed young Koreans to new ideas. Nor could they keep out the Japanese and Russians who opened businesses and indulged in political intrigue. China's period of dominance came to an end in 1894 when the Tonghaks revolted. A panicky government in Seoul called on Chinese assistance but before troops could arrive Korean officials were able to negotiate with the Tonghaks, promising to look into their grievances. Although no longer needed the Chinese forces arrived anyway. Tokyo, concerned that China would consolidate its hold on the peninsula, sent its troops. This led to the Sino-Japanese War in which Japan's modern army and navy inflicted punishing defeats on the Chinese and drove them out of Korea.

The Japanese victory eliminated China, in the competition to control Korea. Tokyo, now in control of events in Seoul, sponsored a reform-minded government that carried out a series of measures known as the Kabo Reforms. These eliminated yangban status, abolished slavery, established equality before the law, prohibited child marriage, allowed widows to remarry, and did away with the civil service exams. A new Western calendar was adopted and the tributary status with China officially came to an end. The Kabo Reforms were enthusiastically enacted by Korean reformers who had been sidelined or exiled for the past decade, including surviving members of the Enlightenment Party. But the reformers, no matter how sincere, were viewed by many as instruments of Japan which was tightening its grip over the country. Anti-Japanese feeling was inflamed when Japanese thugs, acting under the direction of Tokyo's minister in Korea, murdered the staunchly anti-Japanese Queen Min, covered her body in kerosene, and burnt it.

Some Koreans sought the help of Russia in freeing the government from Japanese control. St Petersburg, eager to extend its influence in the peninsula, obliged. In early 1896, a pro-Russian faction at court spirited King Kojong out of the palace, past the watchful eyes of the Japanese, and off to the Russian legation. The king ruled from the Russian legation protected by Cossacks. This pathetic state of affairs encouraged a group of Korean progressives to form the Independence Club led by the American-educated Yun Ch'iho, and later joined by Sŏ Chaep'il, an 1884 coup leader who returned from exile in the USA. The Club called for modern representative government, and an independent foreign policy. Under its influence the country was renamed the Great Korean Empire; King Kojong became Emperor Kojong. This was a final break with the Sino-centric tributary system, and symbolically placed Korea on equal footing with its imperial neighbours. In another break with tradition and to emphasize Korea's cultural independence from its neighbours its newspaper was printed in *Hangul*, not in Chinese characters. However, before the Independence Club could carry out further reforms, Emperor Kojong and his conservative advisers, fearing it was acquiring too much power, had it banned; its leaders were arrested or, like Sŏ, fled abroad.

From empire to colony

Despite its new imperial status Korea, or the Great Korean Empire as it was now called, was a weak, politically divided state led by a vacillating, indecisive king now titled emperor. His government had to deal with the imperial ambitions of Japan and Russia, both keen on securing control over the country and denying it to the other. Some Koreans looked to the United States to balance the power of Japan and Russia. But despite a strong American missionary presence, Washington showed little interest in the country. Tokyo made a secret offer to St Petersburg to accept Japanese control over Korea in exchange for Japanese recognition of Russian interest in Manchuria. But this was rejected by the Tsarist government. Then, in 1904, Japanese forces carried out a surprise attack on the Russians in Manchuria, launching the Russo-Japanese War. When Japan emerged victorious in 1905, Russia conceded Korea and much of Manchuria as a Japanese sphere of influence. President Theodore Roosevelt, who brokered the peace settlement, tacitly gave Tokyo a free hand in Korea in return for its recognition of the American presence in the Philippines. Britain too, which had formed an alliance with Japan in 1902, recognized Tokyo's paramount interests in the peninsula. Consequently, with the blessings of the great powers, Japan declared Korea a protectorate in 1905. Western states closed their embassies and Korea became all but in name a Japanese possession. Korea sent representatives to a peace conference in The Hague in 1907 to protest Japanese violation of its sovereignty, but the outside world showed little concern for its plight.

For five years, Korea was nominally independent but in reality power shifted from the Korean monarch and prime minister to a Japanese resident-general, and from the Korean cabinet ministers to their Japanese advisers. In 1907, the army was disbanded, and when Kojong began to act too independently he was forced to abdicate in favour of his mentally incompetent and easily manipulated son Sunjong. In 1910, Korea was formally annexed. Some Koreans, viewing the Japanese as agents of progress, supported the annexation of their country, some resigned themselves to the inevitable, some violently resisted. The last formed 'righteous armies' which carried out a war of resistance from 1907 to 1910. About 10,000 were killed fighting the vastly superior Japanese forces.

It is easy to look back at these last years of Korea as a sovereign country and view it as an ineffective, pathetic, and even hopelessly backward state. Yet the brief Great Korean Empire enacted legal reforms, established the basis for a modern education system, carried out a systematic land survey, and signed contracts with foreign investors to construct modern infrastructure. In 1899, for instance, the first railway opened linking Seoul with the port of Inchon (Inch'ŏn) and the first electric street cars began operation in the capital (Figure 5). Many individual Koreans began embracing change: starting newspapers, establishing modern schools, opening businesses. A small number of intellectuals absorbed Western ideas, reading Western political, economic, and scientific works, usually in Japanese translations.

Many educated Koreans, using the new media such as newspapers, began to re-examine what it meant to be Korean and

5. Seoul street car, 1899.

the place of Korea in the world. They began to place their society in the context of world not just East Asian history. They adopted the modern idea that history was a linear march of progress, and they feared that their country had fallen behind. Many Korean intellectuals felt their task was to direct Korea's efforts to modernize and strengthen itself if it was to survive.

Korean writers began to define themselves as members of a nation in the modern sense. Early manifestations of modern nationalism include the Independence Club formed in 1896, and the work of Sin Ch'aeho, who wrote a work on Korean history in 1905 as the story of a nation. But this new identity competed with or was combined with other new categories for labelling themselves. As a result of their encounter with Western ideas they began identifying as 'Easterners' and as Asians. Some embraced Pan-Asianism, an idea developed by some Japanese thinkers that all the peoples of the Pacific Rim of Asia should cooperate in challenging the dominance of the West, and that Japan should lead them in this effort. Pan-Asianism was influenced by social Darwinism, especially its German form that emphasized the history as a struggle for survival among the races. Other Koreans incorporated social Darwinism in their ideas of nationalism—history as a struggle among nations for survival.

Modernization under colonial rule

Korea's colonial experience was in many ways typical of Asian and African peoples in the age of imperialism. Japan, like other colonial powers, directed the development of Korea for its own benefit not for that of Koreans. Koreans were treated as inferior subjects, their traditions were often denigrated, and they were excluded from positions of authority. It was a humiliating experience. Nonetheless, some embraced the new opportunities that were made available and accepted the claim by the Japanese that they were bringing progress and enlightenment. Many Koreans were active agents, not just passive victims, of the colonial administration, serving as police and holding minor positions in the bureaucracy. Some became admirers of Japanese culture and took pride in being part of the great, rising Japanese Empire. Others resisted, some violently, some more passively; several thousand became exiles and plotted the overthrow of colonial rule from abroad.

In other ways Korea's colonial experience was unusual. Unlike many colonial subjects, such as the peoples of Indochina, India, or West Africa who were ruled by a distant and alien nation, Koreans were governed by a familiar, culturally related neighbour. Although warrior-dominated Japan had a very different social system from Korea, it shared traditions of Buddhism, Confucianism, and a long history of borrowing from China. Furthermore, Korea's colonial experience was unusual in its intensive and intrusive nature. Europeans often ruled indirectly working with local African chiefs, or rajas or emirs, but in Korea all authority was concentrated in the centralized Japanese administration. By the 1930s about a quarter of a million Japanese civilian, military, and police personnel were employed in Korea. This was about the same as the number of British in India, which had more than fifteen times the population, ten times as many as the French in Vietnam, a colony with a similar population to Korea. While an Indian or African peasant might only rarely encounter a British or French colonial official, ordinary Koreans encountered them every day—the Japanese schoolteacher, the postal clerk, the village policeman. The police had the power to judge and sentence for minor offences, to collect taxes, to oversee local irrigation works, even to inspect businesses and homes to see that health and other government regulations were being enforced. It was a top–down administration with all officials, police, and military directly answerable to the governor-general, always a Japanese military man appointed by Tokyo. Koreans served mainly in the lower ranks of the bureaucracy and were excluded from any meaningful participation in decision-making.

Korea's geopolitical situation also made its colonial experience different. The Japanese saw the peninsula as occupying a strategic position—first as protecting the homeland from foreign invasion, second as a springboard for advancing into Manchuria and the Chinese mainland. It therefore carried on infrastructure and industrial development to serve these purposes. Tokyo, for example, built an extensive railway system with nearly as many miles of track as in all of China; its primary purpose was to transport troops from Japan to Manchuria as well as Korean goods to ports. After 1930, it developed the mineral-rich north as a major industrial base, leaving Korea with a more developed infrastructure and more industrial plants than most other colonies.

Another peculiar feature of Japan's rule was its assimilationist policy. Other colonial powers, especially the French, had sought to promote cultural integration among elements of the educated elite, but Japan conducted a massive, if inconsistent, attempt to forcibly assimilate the entire population into Japanese culture. Officially the policy was based on the fiction that the two peoples were originally one but had become separated. The Japanese had progressed while the Koreans had stagnated. It was now the duty of Tokyo to reunite with their backward Korean relatives and absorb them into Japanese society. But this policy, which meant trying to erase Korea's culture and identity, was contradicted by the practices of carefully segregating Koreans and Japanese, building different schools, dividing cities into separate neighbourhoods etc., and treating Koreans as an inferior people with a subordinate role in the empire.

Colonial modernity

Before 1910, Koreans began the process of modernization; after 1910 the process accelerated but it was directed by the Japanese colonial authority primarily to serve Japanese interest.

Nonetheless, many Koreans benefited economically. A new middle class emerged: teachers, doctors, accountants, businessmen, bankers, and civil servants in the colonial bureaucracy who were connected to the modern world. They wore Western-style clothes, read newspapers, magazines, and foreign books in translation. They sent their children to modern schools where the curriculum included science and maths as well as civics, history, and literature. This new middle class included a group of modern entrepreneurs. The old stigma against commerce was diminishing and many educated Koreans entered businesses of all kinds. Some operated rice mills, textile plants, trucking companies, and banks. This small Korean business class worked closely with their Japanese counterparts, but they had their own separate chamber of commerce in Seoul. Some of these such as Kim Sŏngsu and his brother Kim Yŏnsu, owners of the Kyŏngbang Textile Company, were of yangban background, a break with the traditional aristocratic avoidance of commerce. Others such as such as Pak Hŭngsik, owner of retail stores and the richest man in colonial Korea, came from a commoner family.

Even among this new middle class, however, men's attitudes towards women changed slowly and few women appeared in public life. Yet for women things were changing too. Many left home to take jobs in factories where they made up a substantial portion of the workforce. And women were getting educated, although the purpose of educating women was not to prepare them for professional life, but for roles as 'wise mothers, good wives', who could better supervise the education of their children. A few women, however, broke from even this changed role, becoming writers, educators, artists, and active in political movements. One of these, Kim Wŏnju, published *Sin Yŏsŏng* (New Woman), a 1920s magazine aimed at the modern woman. The title 'New Woman' came from the popular term for modern Korean women who entered the professions, became politically active, and rebelled against the limitations that society had placed on them—women such as Pak Kyŏngwŏn, the first Korean woman aviator.

Yet most Koreans benefited little from this colonial modernization. Korean workers earned only a third of the wages of their Japanese counterparts and were seldom allowed to rise to management levels. Labour strikes and other forms of unrest were common until repressive measures in the 1930s made any form of collective action extremely difficult. Education expanded but it was designed to meet the requirements for educated labour. Few upper-level schools were built. In fact, the pace of educational development was so slow that non-accredited private schools grew rapidly in the 1920s–1930s to meet demand.

Despite the growth of industry and urbanization, Korea remained a rural society. Three-quarters of the population were peasants, and for the most part this group experienced the greatest hardship from colonial modernization. Landownership declined, and most peasants became tenant farmers. When the Japanese carried out systematic land surveys many peasants lost land because they could not prove ownership, which was often based on custom. As a result, most of the land fell into the hands of rich yangban who took advantage of their knowledge of law and of government regulations. Eventually, about 2 per cent of rich families possessed over half the land. Most farmers either owned no land or not enough to support a family. To survive they had to rent land from a big landowner or work in his fields. Small farmers were required to cultivate some crops for the market and then found that the increasing commercialization of agriculture subjected them to sharp market fluctuations. They frequently accumulated high levels of debt. Population growth also put pressure on the land. Among the worst-off farmers were those who moved into the mountain forests, where they squatted on public land. They would burn trees and bushes, sow and harvest a crop, then move on to another field, barely eking out a precarious existence. This contributed to the deforestation of the country as traditional customs that protected the woodlands broke down. By the end of colonial rule, the barren mountainsides of the country came to symbolize to some the rape of the country under foreign occupation.

Of all the hardships experienced by rural Koreans few were recalled with greater bitterness than the disappearance of rice from their tables. Rice production went up under colonial rule; however, this was to supply the Japanese homeland. Cheap millet, contemptuously regarded as 'coarse grain', was imported from Manchuria for Koreans while the rice they grew went to the Japanese. By the end of the colonial period, Korea had become a land where the majority of the population were farmers who owned no land or not enough to support themselves, who were burdened with high rents, high land taxes, and could not even eat the rice they grew. This resulted in peasant unrest that would come out in the open when colonial rule ended in 1945.

The birth of modern Korean nationalism

Nationalism emerged as a powerful emotional force among the people during colonial rule. At the start of colonial rule in 1910, the concepts of nation and nation-state were still new ones largely confined to small circles of thinkers and people who had been educated abroad or in Western-run mission schools. By 1945 most Koreans had come to see themselves as members of a Korean nation. Modern nationalist sentiment and nationalist movements emerged in almost all of the colonies during the first half of the 20th century in the form of anticolonialism. It often served as a means of integrating diverse ethnic, religious, and other groups into a single community based on the colonial territory. However, Korea already had a long experience as a territorially stable, centralized state with an ethnically and culturally homogeneous population. For that reason nationalism was able to quickly become a popular and powerful force.

The first great outburst of Korean nationalism was the March First Movement of 1919. At the end of the First World War President Wilson declared the principle of national self-determination. This excited many victims of imperialism across the world. Koreans were among the first to be animated by this promising turn of international events. In late February representatives of various Protestant, Chŏndogyo (as the Tonghak religion was renamed), and Buddhist groups decided to issue a declaration of independence, as a kind of peaceful protest statement in a park in Seoul. What happened instead was a largely spontaneous mass protest involving hundreds of thousands of Koreans in every province and city in Korea. Although mostly peaceful it was violently suppressed by the Japanese; several thousand were killed, thousands arrested. Taken by surprise, an embarrassed Japanese government changed its colonial policy toward a more liberal one in the 1920s. Upon annexing Korea in 1910, the colonial authorities had closed most Korean newspapers and publications, as well as many private schools. But in the wake of the March First Movement they allowed newspapers and journals in the Korean language, as well as a number of private organizations that promoted Korean culture. It was in this limited space that a great flowering of Korean literature, political thought, and historical studies flourished.

The Korean nationalist movement, however, soon became ideologically divided. Moderates sought a gradual approach toward independence. These gradualists, such as the influential writer Yi Kwangsu, had a free and independent Korea as their aim but saw it as a long-term project. Korea had to first improve itself by working within the boundaries permitted by the Japanese colonial administration to modernize the country. A major task was to educate the still 'backward' people. Only when the people achieved a sufficient level of maturity and 'modernity' would Korea be ready to join the ranks of sovereign states. Moderates, including much of the new middle class of businessmen, educators, writers, and journalists, established schools, newspapers, and self-improvement societies that they believed would lead the ignorant masses into the modern world. Thus, they were able to persuade themselves that they were forwarding the independence movement by cooperating with the colonial occupiers. In seeking ways to create a modern society they looked for models not just in Japan but in the Western countries of Europe and America. This was especially true of the Christians, a group disproportionally represented among moderate nationalists. With their ties to Western missions and unease with the Japanese imperial cult they were especially open to Western concepts of modernity.

Many Korean nationalists turned to more radical paths to achieve liberation and to establish Korea as a member of the international community of modern sovereign states. They took ideas from many sources, such as anarchism, but none was as influential as communism. At first few Koreans had any awareness of communism. This changed with the Bolshevik Revolution of 1917, Lenin's denunciation of imperialism, and the offers of the new Bolshevik regime in Russia to provide assistance to colonial peoples in the struggle to free themselves from foreign rule. When Lenin called an international conference of the Toilers of the East in Moscow in 1922, Koreans were the largest group to attend. In a complex, confusing world Marxism-Leninism had much to offer. It provided an explanation for the country's weakness, its poverty, and its victimization at the hands of the Japanese. It was an all-embracing philosophy, which like Neo-Confucianism presented a clear path to a virtuous, harmonious, prosperous society. In fact, Korean Marxists were very much like their Neo-Confucian ancestors, coming back from abroad with a prescription to cure society's ills and lead it to a bright future. Young Koreans formed several Marxist 'study clubs'. In 1925 they made four attempts to organize a Korean Communist Party; each time the Japanese police quickly arrested its members. Nonetheless, an underground domestic communist movement continued.

Not all radical nationalists fully adhered to or understood orthodox Marxism-Leninism, but they shared the scorn for the elitist views of the moderate nationalists whom they saw as self-serving Japanese collaborators. All radical nationalists, whether or not Marxist, viewed the struggle for independence as inseparable from the internal struggle to liberate the people from exploitation by the elite. Some of them formed labour and peasant organizations, others confined their activities to writing and waiting for an opportune time to bring about liberation of the nation and its people. Korean communists saw themselves as part of an international movement and in theory identified with the global struggle of the working class. Yet the Marxist emphasis on class identity over nation never replaced the passionate nationalism of its Korean adherents.

Many Korean nationalists were based abroad. However, rather than a unified movement they were divided by ideology, disagreements on tactics, and by geography. Most independence movements among Asians and Africans during the heyday of colonialism had an important overseas base of operation: London, Paris, Switzerland, New York, etc. Korean exiles were scattered all over the globe. Some worked in Tokyo before the repression of the 1930s made that no longer viable. Others were in Shanghai, Manchuria, western China, Siberia, Hawaii, and the US mainland. The efforts of these globally dispersed groups were largely uncoordinated. In 1919, they tried to combine their efforts and formed the Korean Provisional Government in Shanghai. Its first president was the American-based nationalist leader Syngman Rhee (Yi Sŭngman). This organization, however, proved too ideologically diverse to be effective. Some Korean exiles carried out terrorist attacks against the Japanese; in one they narrowly missed assassinating Japanese Emperor Hirohito. During the Second World War exiles in China fought with the Chinese.

Kim Ku led a Korean Restoration Army with several thousand fighters that fought with the Kuomindang regime based on Chungking. A larger number served with the Chinese Communist Party under its leader Mao Zedong. These were organized in 1942 as the Korean Voluntary Army.

Even before the war, several thousand Koreans were fighting the Japanese in the mountains of Manchuria along the northern border of Korea. Drawn from the hundreds of thousands of Koreans who had emigrated to Manchuria, they served under the Chinese Communist Party. One of these young Korean guerrilla fighters was Kim Sŏngju, whose father had settled in Manchuria from the Pyongyang area when he was 9 years old. Kim joined the Chinese Communist resistance to the Japanese sometime around the age of 20, changing his name to Kim Il Sung (Kim Ilsŏng). At the young age of 25 he led a small guerrilla raid on the border city of Poch'ŏnbo, briefly capturing it from the Japanese. This raid in June 1937 made Kim Il Sung modestly famous, since it was widely reported in the Korean language press. Overall, these guerrilla raids were little more than a nuisance to the well-organized and equipped Japanese military. Tokyo destroyed most of these Korean and Chinese guerrillas in Manchuria in a 1939–40 anti-insurgency campaign. The survivors, including Kim Il Sung, fled across the Soviet border.

Wartime totalitarianism

Korea's colonial experience took an increasingly authoritative and coercive turn in the 1930s. As the Great Depression engulfed much of the world, and the international trading system was replaced by a rise in protectionist policies, the Japanese government in Tokyo shifted in an increasingly militaristic, ultra-nationalist direction. In 1931, the Japanese began a takeover of Manchuria, creating a puppet state in the huge, resource-rich region. Six years later the Japanese launched a large-scale invasion of China, capturing its capital Nanjing in 1938. After the start of the war with China in 1937, Japan moved in an increasingly totalitarian direction at home and in Korea.

As the Japanese government moved in a more ultra-nationalist, expansionary direction it began insisting that Koreans actively support the goals of the empire. From 1935 all Koreans were required to worship at Shinto shrines. From 1937 they were required to recite the Oath of Subjects of the Imperial Nation. Schoolchildren began their day by bowing in the direction of the Imperial Palace in Tokyo. The colonial government closed Korean organizations, replacing them with large-scale state-sponsored ones. Writers belonged to the writers' association designed to direct their efforts toward wartime propaganda, young people to the Korean Federation of Youth Organizations. In 1940, the entire country was organized into 350,000 Neighbourhood Patriotic Organizations, each with ten households. These new organizations were used by the state to collect contributions, carry out rationing, and organize people for 'volunteer' labour. Through them almost everyone was enlisted for tasks such as building airstrips and collecting useful materials for war production.

By 1940, the colony was taking on the character of a totalitarian state where all activity was directed towards the goals of the state. When the war expanded in late 1941 from a conflict with China to one with the United States and the British Empire, hundreds of thousands of Koreans were conscripted to work in Japan. School terms were shortened so that students could do voluntary labour and many young people were among those sent to Japan as labourers. In fact, by 1945 a sizeable portion of the total labour force in Japan was Korean (Figure 6). A most tragic development that remains a sore point between Korea and Japan today was the use of up to 200,000 young Korean women as 'Comfort Women'. Recruited under false pretences they were forced to serve as prostitutes for Japanese troops.

6. Recruitment of Korean workers for Japan, Kyŏngsang Province, c.1940.

Returning home in disgrace, many had to carry the shame for their entire lives.

The mass mobilization of the people for the war effort was accompanied by an attempt at forced assimilation. As part of the process of making what one official slogan referred to as 'Korea and Japan—One Body', limitations were placed on the use of Korean. From the late 1930s the use of the Korean language in schools was restricted further and further until students could be punished for speaking it. Korean-language newspapers were shut down and virtually all publications in Korean ceased. In 1940, Koreans were required to change their names to Japanese ones. This 'loss of names' was especially traumatic in Korean society where the veneration of ancestors and maintaining family lines was so important. It was more than a loss of identity, it was a betrayal of one's ancestors.

Ultimately, Tokyo's efforts at assimilation were not very successful. A few Koreans accepted the reality of being part of the Japanese Empire and sought to adopt Japanese culture. Yet no matter how hard they tried, Koreans were not accepted by Japanese as one of them. Nor did they mix socially. Belonging to an insular, racially exclusive society, the Japanese kept apart from Koreans and intermarriage was rare. Rather than creating harmony and unity between the two peoples, colonial policies and attitudes did quite the opposite; they contributed to the emergence of a passionate Korean nationalist sentiment.

Chapter 4
From colony to competing states

As the Second World War came to an end, most Koreans hoped that their nation would be an independent and prosperous state. Instead, during the short span between the closing days of the Second World War in the summer of 1945 and the ceasefire in the Korean War in the summer of 1953 events took a turn that few, if any, had expected.

Korea became both free of Japanese colonial rule and simultaneously partitioned into two occupation zones by the United States and the Soviet Union. For the first time in over a millennium the peninsula was politically divided. Occurring at the very moment of its liberation this came to be regarded among almost all Koreans as one of the great tragedies and discontinuities in their history. Out of these occupation zones the Americans and Soviets supporting different ideological factions among Korean nationalists created two separate states—the Republic of Korea (South Korea) and the Democratic People's Republic of Korea (North Korea). In just a few years, Korea became two societies with different leaderships, political systems, and geopolitical orientations. When North Korea attempted to reunify the country in 1950, foreign powers again intervened in Korean affairs; the result was a costly conflict that left the peninsula still divided.

Liberation and Division

When the Japanese surrendered on 15 August 1945 Koreans throughout the country danced in the streets and celebrated for several days. It was generally assumed that the Allied liberation of their country would mean immediate independence. In the days between the Japanese surrender and the arrival of Allied troops, Koreans across the country formed hundreds of 'People's Committees' (*inmin wiwŏnhoe*). These were ad hoc groups that mostly dealt with immediate tasks such as securing food supplies and maintaining basic order. Although the name 'People's Committees' suggested to some outsiders, especially to the Americans, that they were communist dominated or inspired, they were in fact mostly spontaneous and represented all sorts of people. On 6 September delegates from these various committees formed the Korean People's Republic. They elected Syngman Rhee, who was still in exile in America, as its president.

Koreans did not realize that the Allies had no intention of giving Korea its independence until after a long period of 'tutelage'. Although they had previously given little thought to Korea, at the Cairo Conference in December 1943 Roosevelt, Churchill, and Chinese leader Chiang Kai-shek agreed that Korea would gain its independence 'in due course' upon the defeat of Japan. Franklin Delano Roosevelt, who like most Americans knew little about Korea, proposed that it be placed under a UN trusteeship for forty years, until Koreans were ready for independence, not appreciating the fact that Koreans had many centuries of experience in being an independent state. Stalin agreed but suggested shortening the period to between twenty and thirty years.

The decision to partition Korea into two occupation zones was made at a hastily called meeting on the night of 10 and 11 August by the State-War-Navy Coordinating Committee in Washington. Four days earlier, the Americans had dropped the atom bomb on

Hiroshima and two days after that the Soviet Union declared war on Japan and began an assault along the northern part of its empire. Fearing that the Soviets were in a position to occupy the entire peninsula, the Americans drew up the proposal to prevent all of it from falling under Soviet control. For reasons that are unclear, Moscow quickly accepted it. The thirty-eighth parallel was chosen, simply because it divided the two zones into equal-sized halves. The decision was made as a temporary measure, by people who were largely ignorant of the country. Unfortunately for the future of Korea, the United States and the Soviet Union, who had agreed to a joint occupation, were quickly heading for a political and ideological rivalry.

The speed with which Koreans had formed local governing committees and the unbridled display of emotion that accompanied liberation indicated just how strongly the people shared a collective sense of national identity and a desire to create an autonomous state. However, the authoritarian nature of the colonial regime had left them with a local leadership who had, willingly or not, compromised with the imperial regime. Nor did they have institutions to create the framework for governance. Christian churches had often become a haven for nationalists, but only 5 per cent of Koreans were members, and many of them too were compromised by collaboration with the colonial regime. There were the communists, but they barely survived as a weak underground organization. Those nationalist leaders with untarnished reputations were in exile and unable to quickly return. As a result, the Allies entered a Korea with a leadership vacuum.

The occupation

Koreans expected to be liberated from occupation. Instead they got new foreign occupiers. If Koreans were not ready for these new occupations, neither were the Soviets nor the Americans.

Both arrived without clear plans or even Korean-language interpreters. The Soviets occupied their zone first, entering Pyongyang on 26 August. Upon their arrival they found that the People's Committees were already carrying on the functions of local government. At first, they worked with them. But many of their members were Christians, including the Pyongyang committee's Cho Mansik, a Christian advocate of non-violence. Pyongyang, the centre of their Soviet administrative zone, was a stronghold of Christianity. Its members were better educated, made up much of the middle class, and were the natural leaders of the community; but they were also strongly anti-communist. Therefore, the Soviets sought partners among the communists. However, the Korean Communist Party was awkwardly headquartered at Seoul, in the American zone, and most of the leadership lived in the south. The local communists in the north were obscure figures, unknown to Moscow; so the Soviets looked to the exile community.

Several weeks into the occupation the Soviets found their candidate for leader in one of these returning exiles: Kim Il Sung. After fleeing to Siberia in 1940, Kim and many of his fellow Manchurian guerrillas had become part of the 25th Red Army's 88th Special Reconnaissance Brigade. When the war ended they tried without much success to return to Korea. Finally, Kim and sixty of his comrades managed a ride on a ship to the port of Wonsan on the East Sea where they disembarked on 19 September. It was his first time in Korea since the age of 12. Wearing Soviet military uniforms, familiar with the Soviet army, speaking some Russian, and with an unimpeachable reputation as anti-Japanese resistance fighters, this small group of former Manchurian guerrillas appeared to the Soviets to be the suitable Koreans they were looking for. Although not the most senior member, Kim Il Sung was the best known and impressed the Russian officers who interviewed him. The occupation authorities almost immediately began promoting him. His big debut came on 14 October when the Soviets organized a massive welcoming ceremony for the Red

Army attended by hundreds of thousands. Kim was given the task of delivering the keynote speech. From then on it became apparent that he was being designated by the Soviets as the leader in their zone of occupation. Many of his partisan companions were placed in key positions.

Early in 1946, the Soviets removed Cho Mansik from his posts and arrested him. Almost all positions in North Korea went to communists. In addition to Kim Il Sung and his guerrilla companions these included hundreds of bilingual Soviet-Koreans from the USSR who provided technical expertise. They were particularly valuable because of their familiarity with Soviet government and party organization. At the same time, thousands of Korean communists returned from China. These so-called 'Yenan Communists' included the prominent leader Kim Tubong, who formed a rival communist party, the New People's Party, which at the insistence of the Soviets merged with the North Korean Branch Bureau, as the Korean Communist Party in the Soviet zone was called. Meanwhile, as the Americans and their allies in the south began to crack down on the communists most of the leaders fled north forming a 'Domestic Communist' faction under the leadership of Pak Hŏnyŏng. Therefore, Kim Il Sung had to share the power with many others but still he was the leader the Soviets promoted.

While after just a few months the Soviets assembled a leadership in the north, the Americans struggled during their three-year occupation to establish order and find Koreans they could comfortably work with. The situation they faced was more complex since their zone included Seoul, the centre of political and intellectual life, with its many competing groups jockeying for power. But the Americans compounded their problems by a series of blunders. Unlike the Soviets, the Americans refused to work with or even acknowledge the People's Committees, falsely believing they were controlled by communists. Nor did they recognize the Korean People's Republic but rather disbanded it.

Instead, the US military commander initially ordered Koreans to continue to obey the Japanese colonial authorities until the new American military government was fully in place. This was meant as only a temporary measure of expediency to ensure order until the Americans could put their own administration in place. Koreans were stunned that they were supposed to obey the oppressors that they had just been liberated from. The Americans quickly realized their mistake and sent the Japanese back to their homeland but they never fully regained the trust of the people they had been sent to govern.

Conservative landowners, businessmen, and former Korean officials in the colonial regime were quick to use the Americans to establish an administration that would protect their interests. A week after the Americans arrived they formed the Korean Democratic Party—a conservative grouping to counter the Korean People's Republic. The Americans appointed these conservatives to an advisory council, and staffed the administrative posts and the top positions in the police force with them. At the same time the US occupation authorities banned the Communist Party; its members as well as other leftists were arrested or fled to the north. However, US officials had an ambivalent attitude toward conservatives whose hold over the south they were fostering. The Americans shared their anti-communism, but they were uncomfortable about their lack of nationalist credentials, their extreme rightist views, and the thuggery of the newly created police forces, and some understood that a Korean administration dominated by landowners represented an obstacle to the popular desire for land reform.

Like the Soviets, the Americans soon looked to the returning exiles for potential leaders. The most prominent was Syngman Rhee, the well-known and respected nationalist who returned to Seoul from America on a US military plane. His dramatic entry suggested an official US endorsement for his leadership; however, he returned to Korea much as did Kim Il Sung, on his own to a country he had not seen in years. On 20 October, just six days after Kim Il Sung made his public debut at the mass rally, Rhee appeared in public introduced by General Hodge. With his fluent English, his staunch anti-communism, his personal charisma, and the energy of a man much younger than his 70 years, the Americans felt they had found their leader much as the Soviets had singled out Kim. Yet Rhee soon proved to be too independent, having no intention of being, or being viewed as, an American puppet.

Rhee shared the anti-communism of the conservatives, yet unlike them he had an unblemished anti-Japanese reputation. As a result, Rhee and the conservatives formed an alliance; they supported him, and he protected them from those Koreans who wanted revenge against collaborators. Uneasy with this alliance, some US officials looked for more moderate leaders. One candidate was the charismatic moderate leftist Yŏ Unhyŏng, who teamed up with Kim Kyusik, a more conservative-leaning moderate. However, any hope that they could form an alternative leadership group to the conservatives was dashed in July 1947 with Yŏ's assassination, most likely engineered by his conservative foes. Desperate, the Americans even turned to another exile, Sŏ Chaep'il, the ageing former leader of the Independence Club. But Sŏ, dying of cancer, came to Korea only to take a look at a homeland he hadn't seen in decades.

The US occupation zone was plagued by labour strikes and student demonstrations. Some of these were instigated by communists, many were simply expressions of frustration and impatience with the way the events were unfolding. Students often protested against placing 'Japanese collaborators' in administrative positions in the newly established secondary schools and colleges, workers wanted higher wages, farmers land. The Americans responded by carrying out thousands of arrests. However, strikes and demonstrations continued, lending a somewhat chaotic nature to the occupation period.

By 1947, this anti-communist alliance of Rhee and the conservatives dominated the bureaucracy of the nascent South Korean state and its security organs. The conservative character of the South was reinforced by the thousands of landlords, businessmen, Christians, and others fleeing from the North, most possessing a passionate hatred of communism. In the process they were creating what could be called the South Korean system. It was a political order dominated by anti-communist, pro-business, economically and socially conservative nationalists whose political views were shaped as much by the authoritarian, ultra-nationalist Japanese colonial regime as by American ideas of liberal democracy.

The emergence of two states

The creation of two states was not a premeditated plan by the two superpowers, nor by any group of Koreans. It was the outcome of the suspicions and rivalry between Washington and Moscow and was aided and abetted by the political polarization among Korean nationalists. A half-hearted effort to create a unified Korea was made by the major powers. The Soviet Union, the USA, China, and Britain met in December 1945 to discuss UN trusteeship, now reduced to five years. The details were to be worked out by an American–Soviet Joint Commission which met in the spring of 1946, but this accomplished little. The Joint Commission met again in the summer of 1947; by then, however, the structures of two different states had already emerged.

Initially Moscow does not appear to have planned to create a separate state in the north. However, in early 1946, the Soviet occupiers began to take steps to construct a Soviet-style political and social order in their sector. Through carefully managed elections they created a People's Committee in February which carried out sweeping reforms. Under the direction of their Soviet supervisors the People's Committee nationalized all industries, a rather easy step since most had been abandoned by their Japanese owners. It instituted an eight-hour day, five-day work week, and minimum wage. Other laws established equality between men and women and made divorce easy. The emerging northern state carried out mass adult education campaigns and enacted compulsory universal education.

The truly revolutionary measure was the land reform carried out by the People's Committee in the spring of 1946. In a country where most people were tenant farmers or agricultural labourers nothing could have done more to win support for the new political and social system the Soviets and their communist allies were establishing. All the property of the big landowners was confiscated; most fled south of the parallel. Their land was redistributed to poor farmers. Heavy land taxes and the small size of the farms meant that their material existence only marginally improved, but peasants were now working their own land.

Over the next two years, as these measures enacted by the People's Committee were fully implemented, the Soviet occupation created a radically new society in the North, one based on equality in which everyone was to address each other as comrade, in which formerly lowly peasants and workers were told they were the new elite of society, and in which the old yangban class that had dominated society for many centuries was gone. But it was also a regimented society that tolerated no dissent. Protest demonstrations, mostly by Christian groups, were brutally repressed. Writers and artists were enlisted as propaganda agents of the state; and much as the Japanese had done in wartime, everyone was organized by profession, or categories such as women or youth, and mobilized for various campaigns directed at state goals. An elaborate security apparatus was developed under the direction of former Soviet police officer Pang Hakse. North Korea soon had all the makings of a Soviet-style totalitarian government except for a prison system; political prisoners were simply sent to the Soviet Union's Gulag. It was only lacking an army. That was created in early 1948 when some of the security forces were converted into the Korean People's Army.

Theoretically the emerging North Korean state was a multiparty one. In practice, all power was in the hands of the North Korean Workers' Party established in 1946. Kim Il Sung only became its head in 1948 but well before that a cult of personality was created around him. His picture appeared in public places alongside Stalin's, songs were written praising his accomplishments as guerrilla fighter and revolutionary, the first university in the North was named after him. Thus, many features of North Korea were already emerging by the time of its independence in 1948: the cult of personality of the leader, the regimentation of society, and the mass mobilization campaigns to achieve development goals.

In the South, state organs were established at a somewhat slower pace. Under the US military government, a new network of schools was established. The US military trained a national constabulary, which became the basis for a national army, and they established an Interim Legislative Assembly to share in governance. By the end of 1947 the US authorities and the Koreans serving them had created the framework for a sovereign state.

The United States had no desire to prolong its occupation in Korea, a place it had only limited interests in, so it turned to the United Nations to resolve the question of independence. The UN formed a Temporary Committee on Korea which decided to hold elections in the spring of 1948. When the Soviet Union refused to cooperate, the UN Temporary Commission held them anyway in the South. Some southerners, such as Kim Kyusik, desperately sought to prevent separate elections, seeing them as making the division permanent. But neither the Americans nor most of the political leaders in the South saw any realistic possibility of compromise with the authorities in the North. In May 1948, South Koreans lined up for hours to elect the leaders of the National Assembly, the first time they had ever directly participated in their government. The members of the National Assembly elected Rhee as president and on 15 August, the third anniversary of the surrender of Japan, they declared the Republic of Korea (ROK). The North carried out its own more supervised elections and declared the Democratic People's Republic (DPRK) on 9 September. The two Korean states were born.

Division and The desire for national unity

The division of Korea did not weaken the sense among Koreans that they were one nation. Outside powers had simply delayed this process of achieving a unified sovereign state but almost all Koreans on both sides of the thirty-eighth parallel regarded eventual unification as necessary and inevitable. The desire for reunification was reinforced by the ethnic nationalism both Koreas promoted. North Korea was officially socialist and part of the international socialist community. It was a Marxist state where class took precedence over nation, at least in theory. But Kim Il Sung and the DPRK leadership were as much nationalists as they were communists, seeing the Koreans as one people united by blood, ancestry, and sharing a common destiny. In South Korea, the state was officially based on liberalism and considered itself part of the anti-communist 'free world' centred in the USA. Yet Syngman Rhee called his ideology *ilmin chuŭi* or 'one peopleism', awkwardly expressing the same concept of a unitary nation bonded by blood ties and history.

In North Korea, the constitution specified that Seoul (which means 'capital' in Korean) was the capital of the Korean nation, Pyongyang just a temporary one. North Korean leaders saw the state as a sort of base camp from which to liberate the rest of the country. Almost immediately after the DPRK was established its leadership asked for Moscow's support in reunifying the country by force. Similarly, in South Korea school textbooks taught children that Koreans were a 'one-blood' people, whose unity under a single state was an unquestionable goal and inevitable development. President Rhee spoke of 'marching north' and unifying the country by force. In 1949 and 1950, the ROK army carried out numerous incursions into the DPRK, anxious to probe defences and preparing for the day it could liberate the North.

While both North and South Korea were committed to reunification, achieving this peacefully hardly seemed possible, since the leadership of each held incompatible visions of modern society. The DPRK was ruled by revolutionaries who were confident that they were on the right side of history and who regarded the landlord and capitalist class which dominated the South as enemies of the Korean people and obstacles for fulfilling the goal of creating a progressive modern nation-state. In the ROK, the state was dominated by conservative landlords and entrepreneurs who hated and feared the communists.

Therefore, unification by force seemed a realistic option to both Koreas. Of the two states, North Korea was in a much better position to do so. Although it had only half the population of the South its leadership had better nationalist credentials. Furthermore, North Korea had carried out land reform and gained the support of the peasants; South Korea had not. The regime in the DPRK was more effective at consolidating its hold over its people and mobilizing them for state goals. North Korea, in contrast to the South, was beginning to lay the foundations for creating a modern industrial state. Already possessing most of Korea's industry and electrical power generation in 1945, it was beginning to further expand its industrial base by implementing a two-year economic plan for 1949–50.

Most importantly the DPRK had the military advantage. It was quickly building a powerful Korean People's Army. With the proclamation of the People's Republic of China in 1949, tens of thousands of Koreans who had fought in the Chinese People's Liberation Army began returning to Korea, providing a large corps of experienced fighters. Moscow was generous in equipping it with artillery, tanks, and other weapons. The South was much weaker militarily. Its army was smaller; and the USA, fearing it would use them to launch an invasion, refused to supply the ROK forces with military planes, tanks, and other offensive weaponry. Therefore, Kim Il Sung and Pak Hŏnyŏng, the South Korean Communist Party leader who had fled to the North, were optimistic about their chances of quickly achieving unification if they invaded the South.

North Korea's leadership was encouraged by turmoil and unrest in the South. In contrast to the organization and discipline in the DPRK, the ROK was semi-chaotic with the government plunged into quarrels between the executive branch headed by Rhee and the independent-minded members of the National Assembly. There was widespread discontent in the countryside over the failure to carry out land reform, and labour unrest in the cities. Students, many influenced by leftist politics, carried out almost constant protests. A major anti-government uprising took place in the island province of Cheju. In October 1948, just a week after the USA transferred its command to ROK officers, the army was assembled at the port of Yŏsu to sail to the island. But instead of putting down the rebellion, the soldiers themselves revolted. Some waved banners calling for the overthrow of their government. Loyal troops were found who were able to put down the mutiny, but only after heavy fighting. Some of the rebel soldiers retreated into the nearby mountains to form guerrilla bands.

Rhee's government responded to all this chaos by mass arrests of real or suspected communist sympathizers and by launching a series of anti-insurgency campaigns in the countryside. Geopolitical insecurity contributed to the anti-communist hysteria of the regime. The DPRK's allies Russia and China were neighbours whereas the Americans were far away, and their support was uncertain. The Rhee administration gradually achieved progress in maintaining public order and in containing and reducing the scale of the guerrilla insurgency. However, discontent from landless peasants, restless workers, and leftist intellectuals who opposed the Rhee regime, regarding it as reactionary and dominated by former Japanese collaborators, was still a threat to its stability.

Under these circumstances the North Korean leaders assumed an invasion of the South would lead to swift victory. Their main task was to persuade Stalin and Mao to back them. Both were initially reluctant, but in early 1950 Stalin changed his mind and gave his blessing and support for a DPRK military invasion; Mao too gave his approval. Kim Il Sung's patrons may have been encouraged by what appeared to be a waning commitment to the defence of the ROK by the United States. The US Congress had reduced aid, and in January 1950, the American Secretary of State in a speech excluded South Korea from its 'defensive perimeter' in Asia. Moscow sent weapons and advisers and helped Pyongyang prepare for the invasion, which was set for late June, just before the start of the monsoon rains.

The Korean War

On 25 June 1950 what the North Koreans call the 'Great Motherland Liberation War' began as planned. The unprepared ROK forces crumbled before the Korean People's Army and in two days the KPA was in Seoul. Panic took hold in the capital, soldiers retreated, thousands of civilians fled in nightmarish scenes of utter chaos. Roads became rivers of families fleeing south ahead of the advancing KPA, men, women, and children, moving mostly on foot carrying whatever they could on their backs (Figure 7). Symbolizing the horror of these hours was the Han Bridge Incident. There was only one bridge across the mighty Han River that formed the southern border of the city. ROK forces, in an attempt to slow the advancing forces, blew it up prematurely while it was packed with escaping civilians, killing hundreds of them.

Had Kim Il Sung's plans worked, in a matter of weeks, if not days, Korea would have been reunified. But the war did not go as Kim and his comrades had expected. The United States, which was

7. South Korean refugees during the Korean War.

caught by surprise, responded as soon as it was able to confirm that a full-scale invasion was under way. On 27 June, President Truman ordered General MacArthur, head of the occupation forces in Japan, to use US air and naval support at his disposal to support the ROK army. The Americans went to the UN to ask for a resolution giving them the authority to intervene. This they received almost immediately. The Soviet Union, which could have vetoed it, was boycotting the UN in protest at the international body's refusal to allow the representatives of the People's Republic of China to replace the Nationalist government's seat at the UN. The USA thus entered the war under the banner of the UN. Eventually some of America's allies joined the UN effort including troops from Britain, Canada, Turkey, the Philippines, Thailand, and Australia. But although it was in theory an international operation, the USA supplied the bulk of the United Nations forces and was in complete command of operations.

Since it would take the American forces some time to mobilize for action, the KPA could still have succeeded if it had achieved the swift victory it had expected. However, the North Korean leadership had made two other miscalculations. The anticipated great uprising of support for the North Koreans did not materialize. Furthermore, the ROK forces after initially retreating in confusion began to put up more resistance than expected. The result was North Korea's Korean People's Army advanced more slowly than planned, providing the UN forces with time to bring in troops. Still by August the North Koreans had taken over all of South Korea except the south-east corner around Busan which became the temporary capital of the ROK. The KPA was unable to advance beyond this defensive perimeter.

In early September, the UN forces under the American military commander General MacArthur landed at Inchon, catching the North Korean army in a classic pincer. Within days the KPA was routed and Seoul was retaken. In early October UN and ROK forces crossed the thirty-eighth parallel to destroy the North Korean regime and reunite the country under their terms. A cautious Moscow was ready to abandon Kim Il Sung, but not Mao Zedong, who warned the Americans against advancing to the Chinese border. When these warnings were ignored Beijing launched a counter-attack in late November driving the UN and ROK forces back over the parallel, capturing Seoul. The Americans in March 1951 retook Seoul and pushed the Chinese back to a line roughly along the old border; there the war stalemated. Negotiations began in July 1951 and continued until 27 July 1953 when a ceasefire was agreed upon.

The Korean War, rather than reunifying the country, made the division permanent. It was one of the greatest single catastrophes in modern Korean history. Relentless American bombing that was accelerated in 1952 left the cities of the North in total ruin. More bombs were dropped on the New York State (or England) sized country than on the entire Japanese Empire in the Second World War. The total military and civilian casualties are unknown but as many as one million of the nine million people may have perished. South Korea did not see the same scale of devastation but, nonetheless, Seoul, which had changed hands four times in less than a year, was largely destroyed. Hundreds of thousands of military personnel and civilians were killed. The UN casualties at perhaps 40,000 were much less but the Chinese lost several times as many soldiers.

In the South the war increased anti-communist sentiment and hatred of the North Korean regime. North Koreans as they liberated South Korean cities and towns set up People's Committees to govern them. They rounded up suspected ROK officials and class enemies, executing many, and promised to redistribute the land to the farmers. Some students and others came forward to serve the new political order; most South Koreans, however, feared and resented the northern occupation. There were some guerrillas who fought for the North, but they were mostly the remnants of those who had fought in the mountains before June 1950, not new recruits. When few young men volunteered to serve in the armed forces they were drafted against their will. Tens of thousands of these impressed soldiers were forced to retreat with the KPA when it was driven back into North Korea, and most were never heard from by their families again. As a result, the brief North Korean occupation mainly generated hatred for the communists rather than support. South Korea, during its brief occupation of the North, demonstrated a similar capacity to alienate rather than win over the local population. Thousands who had served in the communist regime were arrested, and the ROK authorities threatened to punish anyone who had collaborated with the communists. That of course, included almost everyone. Furthermore, they announced that illegally appropriated land would have to be given back to the rightful landlords.

Both Kim Il Sung and Syngman Rhee ended the war firmly entrenched in power and their regimes in tighter control over their peoples. Yet despite the enormous military sacrifices of their benefactors both felt betrayed by them. Moscow responded to

Kim Il Sung's desperate calls for help following the Inchon landing by urging him to retreat north of the DPRK border, showing a willingness to abandon his regime. The Chinese saved it but marginalized him during the conflict. Their interest was in maintaining the DPRK as a buffer state between the People's Republic of China and the USA and its Asian allies, not in helping to reunify the country. Rhee, too, felt that the Americans had failed to push the war to victory, instead settling for the status quo of a divided Korea. He never disguised his resentment at the Americans for accepting the ceasefire, which went into effect without his signature.

The years immediately after the end of the colonial period in many ways resembled those before the Japanese annexation. Koreans struggled to come to terms with a rapidly changing situation but found that to a considerable extent their fate was in the hands of great powers. China, the Soviet Union, and the United States acted much as imperial China, imperial Russia, and imperial Japan had in the late 19th and early 20th centuries, intruding in Korean affairs—aligning with, supporting, and aggravating the division among political factions. This time the result of internal conflicts and external interventions led not to the loss of sovereignty but to the creation of two rival states, each to some degree dependent on powerful foreign patrons. The Korean War did not change this situation but rather made it more permanent.

Chapter 5
Competing states, diverging societies

By 1953 almost all Koreans had accepted that they belonged to a single nation united by blood, culture, history, and destiny. However, the end of the Korean War left them divided into two states. Each state shared the same goal of creating a prosperous, modern, unified Korean nation-state that would be politically autonomous and internationally respected. The leadership of each saw the division as temporary and themselves and the state they governed as the true representative of the aspirations of the Korean people, and the legitimate successor to the pre-colonial state. Each state saw itself as in competition with the other to demonstrate that it deserved to represent the entire Korean nation and to be in the better position to reunify the country. Yet while sharing many of the same goals they followed very different paths to reach them and thus they became ever more divergent societies.

At first North Korea appeared to be the more successful of the two states in building a modern, militarily strong, self-reliant industrial state. It rapidly recovered from the Korean War and in two decades became the most urbanized and industrialized country in Asia after Japan. South Korea after an unpromising start characterized by political corruption and instability, and seemingly intractable poverty, entered a period of high economic growth after 1961, transforming itself into an industrial nation under an authoritarian military government. South Korea's trajectory of development was the reverse of North Korea's. Its economic development was floundering when the North was roaring ahead, then it began speeding up when the North was slowing down. In the 1980s the South began transition into a democratic society as the totalitarian leadership of the North was evolving into a family-run state; and the South became more globally engaged as the North was becoming internationally isolated.

North Korea's path of modernization and rapid development

For at least the first decade after the Korean War, the DPRK was the more successful of the two Koreas in the competition to establish itself as the legitimate leader of all the Korean nation. Kim Il Sung was able to consolidate his control over the state and the state's control over society. At the same time his regime carried out a rapid economic modernization, building up an industrial base, expanding education, improving health care, all the while achieving a high degree of autonomy from its patrons: the Soviet Union and China. By any measure it was an impressive achievement.

Within a month of the 27 July 1953 ceasefire Kim and his former Manchurian guerrilla partisans began to eliminate their rivals in the leadership of the ruling Korean Workers' Party. In a series of Stalinist show trials the leaders of the domestic communists admitted to being agents of the American imperialists and their southern Korean collaborators. All were promptly executed except the most prominent member, Pak Hŏnyŏng. He was dropped from the Party leadership and quietly arrested and executed two years later. Another major shake-up took place in 1956 when, emboldened by Khrushchev's denouncing the crimes of Stalin and his cult of personality at a secret session of the Soviet Communist Party in February that year, Pak Ch'angok, a prominent Soviet-Korean, and Ch'oe Ch'angik, a leader of the Yenan faction, challenged Kim Il Sung. The challenge failed; Kim removed them from power. In 1957, Kim Il Sung carried out a massive reorganization of the Korean Workers' Party. The result was a three-year purge in which tens of thousands of members whose loyalty to the regime was considered suspect were expelled from the Korean Workers' Party and arrested. Not only Pak and Ch'oe but almost all leaders of the Party who were not from the ex-Manchurian guerrilla faction were removed from office, imprisoned, and in many cases executed.

This massive purge, which resembled the Great Purges Stalin carried out in the Soviet Union in the 1930s, went much further than eliminating potential rivals in the Party. The regime divided the entire population of Korea into three categories: loyal, wavering, and hostile. These were based not only on individual actions but on family backgrounds. Anyone whose family had served in the Japanese colonial administration, been a landlord, owned a business, or had relatives in the South was classified as hostile—up to a third of the population. About 20 per cent, mainly those with untarnished worker or peasant background and who had demonstrated their support of the regime, were placed in the loyal group and the rest in the wavering group. These categories became permanent and inherited. State decrees prevented those from hostile backgrounds from living in the capital or near the border with the ROK. Many were relocated to the remote and impoverished north-east.

Later in the late 1960s these three groupings were subdivided further into *sŏngbun*, a series of graded categories from the most to least loyal. These were also based on family as well as personal background. Those who fought in the mountains with Kim Il Sung or were related to him were at the very top. Thus, North Korea created a system of inherited social ranks, resembling that of pre-modern dynastic Korea but even more elaborate. Family backgrounds were a factor in determining status in other communist societies, but the DPRK's elaborate and rigid *sŏngbun* system was without precedent in the modern world.

By the early 1960s, Kim Il Sung and his Manchurian guerrilla companions were in total control. There was a further smaller-scale purge in 1967. Thereafter, the entire leadership of North Korea consisted of this group, including their family members and their patrons. They were mostly Koreans with only a modest formal education, who grew up in Manchuria not in Korea, men with little exposure to the larger world. They were among the least educated, least cosmopolitan group to dominate any modern society.

Simultaneously, the Kim Il Sung regime focused on building a modern industrial economy. From 1953 to 1956, with assistance from their Soviet, Eastern European, and to a lesser extent Chinese allies, the North Koreans rebuilt their cities, their industrial plants, and their infrastructure. Mass mobilization campaigns put almost every available citizen to work for this effort with impressive results. At the same time the state consolidated private farms into state-owned 'cooperatives' in which peasants became salaried employees working the land they once owned. This effort was largely completed by 1957. So North Korean farmers within a decade of becoming landowners again became agricultural labourers, this time for the state (Figure 8). By then the government had taken over the last small private businesses, completing the socialization of the economy.

In 1957, the regime launched a five-year plan to expand industrial development. Initially modelled on the Soviet five-year plans, after Mao began his Great Leap Forward in 1958 Kim modified the plan to resemble it. Following the Chinese leader, he raised his production goals, consolidated the collective farms into larger, more self-sufficient units, and sent officials to the countryside to learn from the people. Like Mao he hoped to achieve heroic advances in modernization by organizing the common people and

8. Kim Il Sung talking with farmers from Kangsŏ County, October 1945.

instilling revolutionary fervour in them. Unlike Mao, however, he
began to modify his plans when they proved unrealistic and
avoided the disaster that China's Great Leap Forward brought
upon the Chinese people. This was followed by a more achievable
but still ambitious Seven-Year Plan for 1961–7. In carrying out his
development plans, Kim, like Stalin, emphasized heavy industry
over consumer goods. Heavy industry would make his country
less reliant on capital goods from his patrons and form the basis
for domestic arms production. Thus, industrialization was
inseparable from the goal of achieving as much autonomy as
possible and becoming a militarily strong state, capable of
reunifying the country.

The regime's plans were too ambitious to be achieved. Nonetheless
North Korea continued to maintain high economic growth rates
into the early 1970s. By that time it was the most urbanized and
industrialized country in Asia after Japan. It had reached a level of
urbanization and general literacy achieved by China only after
2010. More importantly, for the leadership, it was outperforming
its rival in the south. While living standards were low, life
improved for most North Koreans. Education expanded and adult
literacy programmes brought literacy to most of the adult

population. The entire population had access to basic health care. Massive housing projects moved the urban population into modern apartments, small and crowded but with indoor plumbing and electricity. The latter reached rural homes as well.

North Korea also achieved a greater degree of political autonomy from its patrons. Kim declined membership in the Comecon, the Soviet Union's economic alliance, and avoided getting too close to China while receiving aid from both Moscow and Beijing. The Sino-Soviet split provided Kim Il Sung with an opportunity to play off the two communist giants, each of which saw strategic advantages in maintaining ties with the DPRK. He briefly abandoned the 'equal distance' approach in mid-1963 when he openly sided with China. Moscow retaliated by cutting aid, which was a blow to Korea's economy. After 1965 relationships were patched up and Pyongyang generally maintained good relations with both Moscow and Beijing for the next three decades. The Kim Il Sung regime had not only gained almost complete control of its people, eliminated possible internal rivals, and come a long way toward building a modern industrial society, it had also achieved mastery over its own affairs without outside interference. In a land whose fate in the previous century had been, to a considerable extent, in the hands of outside powers, the last was a notable achievement.

South Korea: uncertain state and then 'economic miracle'

During the first decade after the Korean War, South Korea under Syngman Rhee appeared to be losing the competition for modernization and development. His regime was characterized by authoritarian rule, pervasive corruption, and only modest recovery and growth despite massive US aid. Yet the Rhee administration had some achievements. Land reform was finally carried out, education was enormously expanded, and thousands of South

Koreans went abroad mostly to the United States for advanced studies, forming a pool of well-trained technocrats when they returned. Rhee was ousted in a student-led protest over the blatantly fraudulent elections of 1960 (Figure 9). There was a short-lived experiment with a parliamentary democracy and then in May of 1961 a military coup led by General Park Chung Hee (Pak Chŏnghŭi). Park and the mostly younger officers who planned the coup were frustrated by what they saw as the corruption and incompetence of the civilian government. They were humiliated at the country's dependence on the United States, which provided over half the funds for the state, and whose 60,000 troops in South Korea assured its security. Most of all,

9. Jubilant Korean students swarm over a tank in Seoul, after a civilian rebellion toppled Syngman Rhee from the presidency, April 1960.

they were alarmed at the apparent success of the DPRK in developing a modern, industrial, and more self-reliant state while their Korea was mired in economic stagnation and reduced to dependency on a foreign power. They felt a real fear that the ROK was losing its sense of legitimacy among many of its own people, a fear stoked by student demonstrations that seemed receptive to Pyongyang's overtures.

The new military-led government of South Korea followed many of the same patterns of development as the North. The government sought to gain more control over society and introduce more discipline and regimentation. It created an elaborate secret police force, the Korean Central Intelligence Agency (KCIA), that maintained a vast network of informants. Citizens were mobilized in campaigns of various sorts, although they were not forced to do uncompensated 'voluntary' labour on public projects. There was a greater emphasis on military readiness and military training was introduced into the schools. The main focus of the new regime was on economic development and this too followed the DPRK in many respects. It nationalized the banks and arrested many of the country's leading businessmen in anti-corruption drives. In 1962, it implemented the First Five-Year Development Plan with well-defined industrial and infrastructural targets.

But the Park government also deviated from the development path of the North in significant ways. After forcing most of the country's leading entrepreneurs to pay hefty fines it enlisted them in the effort at pulling the country out of poverty. Lee Byung Chull (Yi Pyŏngch'ŏl), the country's richest businessman, was made the head of an economic advisory council. The state set the goals, then channelled loans on favourable terms to private businesses that competed to complete them. The state also assisted companies with tax breaks, export assistance, favourable rates on state-owned railroads, utilities, and in other ways. But state help was based on the performance of private companies. Those like Hyundai or

Ssangyong that proved efficient were favoured over their less effective competitors. These favoured companies grew into giant conglomerates known as *chaebŏls*. To promote efficiency Park made sure there were at least two competing firms in each sector. His formula—combining private enterprise with state planning and direction—proved highly successful.

South Korea's development also differed from that of the DPRK by creating an export-oriented economy. Park, like Kim, hoped to eventually develop an industrial base that could support an arms industry and free itself from dependency on its patron, the United States. Like Kim, Park spoke of the need for self-reliance. However, lacking technical know-how and capital for heavy industry he opted to focus on consumer industries for the export market. The first five-year plan emphasized textiles, footwear, wigs, and other low-tech, labour-intensive industries for overseas markets. The state also encouraged foreign investment especially from the United States and Japan. Allowing the Japanese to invest heavily in the economy was highly controversial. When Park signed a peace treaty and established full diplomatic relations with Japan in 1965 it ignited mass protest demonstrations so large that they posed a threat to his regime. These mostly student-led protests were based on real fears that Korea would once again become an economic appendage of its former colonial master. Yet the regime's decision to override nationalist sentiment meant that Japanese investment flowed into the country at a time when rising labour costs in Japan made transferring production to its next-door neighbour a practical move. South Korea proved to be an attractive place not only for Japanese but also for American and Western European firms. Park offered them a variety of tax incentives, a low-wage but educated workforce, and state assurances that it would crack down on any labour unrest.

South Korea also differed from North Korea in lacking the degree of political autonomy North Korea achieved in the 1950s. It remained dependent on Washington, which held a partial veto over its policies. American pressure, for example, forced Park to return the government to civilian rule. Taking off his military uniform he ran for and was elected as president in 1963. And although his regime maintained much of the character of an authoritarian police state there were opposition parties, a moderately free press, and some tolerance of the frequent anti-government student demonstrations. This along with independent Christian churches, an array of private organizations, and interest groups made South Korea a more pluralistic society, one in which the state dominated but did not totally control.

Under the Park regime the ROK never achieved the level of freedom from outside control that the DPRK did. Yet South Korea began to economically outperform its northern rival. By the end of the 1960s the economy was growing fast, probably faster than that of the North, and living standards were higher. Sometime, at least by the mid-1970s, if not earlier, South Korea had surpassed the North by every measure of economic strength and well-being of its citizens—education, nutrition, housing, health, and GDP per capita.

The endless conflict

The great issue of national reunification was left unresolved by the Korean War. Neither North nor South saw a division as anything but a temporary situation. South Korea's position at first was mainly defensive. It sought to be prepared if the North attempted to invade again by building up its military and through its alliance with the United States which kept troops along the Demilitarized Zone (DMZ) and in bases throughout the ROK. The USA supplied the ROK forces with equipment and training. By the early 1960s, with 600,000 in its forces plus reserve units South Korea had one of the world's larger militaries. North Korea's during the first decade after 1953 concentrated the DPRK's energies on recovery, the consolidation of the regime, and economic development. But these were done with reunification in mind. Industrial development was aimed at better preparing the country for a resumption of the conflict and at impressing the people of the South that it represented the path to a future unified nation-state.

North Korea began to divert more of its resources to military preparation after 1962 when it began its 'equal emphasis' policy of simultaneously expanding economic and military development. Most of the adult population was given some sort of military training; a significant proportion were on active reserve. Compulsory military training was lengthened until it was often more than ten years. So many men were in the armed forces that eventually the DPRK had a larger military than the ROK despite having only half its population. By the 1970s, it had the largest percentage of its citizenry in active service of any state in the world. The country was fortified, with many miles of underground tunnels designed to withstand American and South Korean bombing. Military production was speeded up through what it called its 'second economy', which produced military vehicles, tanks, artillery, firearms, ammunition. Eventually this was extended to include the production of chemical, biological, and nuclear weapons.

Military drills and the language of military readiness pervaded North Korean society. Kindergarten children practised with toy guns, older schoolchildren with real ones. The country was on a constant war alert. News reports constantly spoke of feverish preparations by the American imperialists and their southern puppets for another attempt to invade the North. Militarism had always been part of the culture of North Korea since the struggle of the Manchurian guerrillas against the Japanese had been used as the model and analogy for all endeavours; it was now amplified. Military drills and preparedness were useful for the regime as a means of disciplining and controlling the population as well as making it ready for the resumption of conflict. But the burden of a poor country devoting so much of its resources to the military made it difficult for the regime to sustain the high levels of growth it achieved in the 1950s and early 1960s.

Meanwhile, in 1964, Kim Il Sung publicly outlined his strategy for reunification. He called for the development of the 'three revolutionary forces'. The first was to develop the revolutionary potential in the DPRK—that is, build up its military, economic, and ideological strength. This included not only industrialization and the expansion of its armed forces, but indoctrination of the population so they would be better prepared for reunification. The second was to strengthen the revolutionary forces in the South. This, Kim admitted, was the mistake of 1950; the people in the South had not yet been fully ready for the revolution. To this end, the policy of the DPRK was to encourage the people of the South to turn on their own government and turn to the North for support. Pyongyang carried this out by sending agents to contact sympathizers in the ROK and help them organize an underground Revolutionary Party for Reunification. Pyongyang felt that there was a real possibility that with its help their southern compatriots would rise up in support of unification under the DPRK. They could appeal to them as the real upholders of Korean nationalist aspirations. After all, the North was successfully modernizing without having foreign troops on its soil or selling out economically to the former Japanese colonial masters.

The third part of the strategy for reunification was promoting 'the international revolutionary forces'. By this Kim meant forcing the withdrawal of American forces in the South, an obvious obstacle to reunification by force, through international pressure. This included gaining the support of the Third World for the DPRK's cause and weakening the USA whenever possible. North Korea supported the North Vietnamese, for example, even sending some pilots in the hopes that, if defeated in Vietnam, the Americans would tire of their military presence in Asia. In the 1970s Pyongyang sought and succeeded in gaining membership in the Non-Aligned Movement. From 1975 to the early 1980s it had enough Third World support for the UN to regularly issue calls for the withdrawal of foreign (meaning American) forces from the Korean peninsula.

For the next thirty years after he first articulated it, Kim Il Sung's foreign policy was built around pursuing these three revolutionary forces with the hope that he would see the reunification of Korea under his leadership. While it was a long-term strategic plan, from time to time his regime sought to speed up the process by stirring up trouble with and within the South. During 1967, the DPRK, hoping to take advantage perhaps of a USA bogged down in Vietnam, ratcheted up tension with a series of 'incidents' along the DMZ involving exchanges of fire. In January 1968, a group of North Korean commandos attacked the Blue House, the presidential mansion in Seoul. They came close to entering before being killed. On the same day the DPRK seized the US navy intelligence ship the USS *Pueblo*; it then held the crew captive. After months of negotiations they were released but the ship was kept as a museum, anchored at the spot where the *General Sherman* had been destroyed. During 1968, teams of commandos sent from the North landed along the east coast of the ROK lecturing the villagers and unsuccessfully trying to gain support for their liberation. In 1969, DPRK forces shot down a US spy plane. North Korea's more aggressive stance, however, made no progress toward reunification. South Koreans showed little interest in being liberated and President Park's elaborate security forces were able to round up and arrest the members of the Revolutionary Party for Reunification.

Following the lead of Beijing, which began talks with the United States in 1971 and welcomed President Nixon in early 1972, Pyongyang initiated negotiations with South Korea. The two countries in July 1972 agreed that all Koreans were one homogeneous people, one nation, that was for the time being politically and ideologically divided but would eventually unite, a view that few Koreans would disagree with. The two sides further agreed that reunification would be done peacefully and without foreign interference. This would take place gradually, starting with a confederation. South Koreans were excited by the possibility of the end of conflict and the movement toward unity. North Korea, however, lost interest in the talks when it became clear that neither Washington nor Seoul had any intention of having US troops withdrawn from the peninsula.

South Korea: authoritarianism, militarism, and heavy industry

In the 1970s, South Korea moved in a more authoritarian, militaristic direction, in some ways resembling the regime in the North. Park altered the constitution, enabling him to run for a third term in 1971 and then, following a surprisingly close vote against Kim Dae Jung (Kim Taejung), a relatively unknown opposition figure, took steps to consolidate his power. In 1972, he declared martial law and then created a new constitution that gave him broader powers. Under this constitution the president was elected by a National Reunification Board whose members Park selected; in this way he was able to remain president indefinitely without direct accountability to the public. He issued a series of presidential decrees clamping down on dissent, making the criticism of the president or the constitution a criminal offence. Political indoctrination increased; cities came to a halt at 5 p.m. and everyone froze to attention as the national anthem blared from loudspeakers. Military training was increased in the schools.

At the same time Park's administration carried out a sweeping rural modernization programme known as the New Village Movement and launched a programme for heavy and chemical industrialization. The latter included construction of the world's largest steel mill, as well as shipyards and petro-chemical plants. The switch from labour-intensive consumer industries to capital-intensive enterprises was viewed with scepticism by South

Korea's American economic advisers. But it reflected Park's desire to both make the country more economically self-reliant and provide the industrial basis for military production. He even carried out secret plans to develop missiles and nuclear weapons; however, these were discovered and vetoed by the USA, which still held great leverage over South Korea.

Yet despite this authoritarian turn, Park never acquired full dictatorial powers. Although weakened there were still opposition political parties, newspapers, and private organizations, many with religious links, that carried on a vocal resistance to his policies. Student demonstrations continued, and there were sporadic outbreaks of labour unrest. A key factor limiting Park's power was South Korea's continued dependency on the USA for military support and as the prime market for its exports. The USA sometimes gave shelter to opponents or threatened reprisals for mistreatment of high-profile dissidents. Furthermore, the state, although repressive, was somewhat constrained by its ideological links with the West. The government in Seoul promoted anti-communism and ultra-nationalism but it also identified with the democratic world and taught liberal democratic ideas of government and society in the schools.

South Korea was, in fact, more connected to the global economy and global culture and its people far less isolated than those of its northern rival. Thousands travelled to the USA for education, millions watched American television, and the economy remained based on trade with the USA, Japan, and Western Europe, all of which had open democratic societies that many South Koreans admired. South Korea's economic development remained primarily export oriented; even its steel industry was designed to be internationally competitive. It was also a more pluralistic society than the North. A factor in the greater pluralism was the rise of Christianity. Christianity grew after 1945 from less than 5 per cent of the population to perhaps one-quarter by the 1980s, making South Korea the second most Christian society in Asia after the Philippines. Most Christian churches avoided political involvement; however, some were involved in labour movements and in political opposition. As was true of the much smaller Christian community under Japanese colonial rule, their international connections gave them some protection from repressive authorities. Traditional respect for education gave university students some cover as well to act as the conscience of society protesting the corruption and abuses of the regime. Labour activists were able to survive despite repression by both government- and industry-employed thugs. The business community, generally supportive of the regime, also had its own interests to protect and sometimes resisted heavy-handed government interference.

In 1979, labour and political unrest broke out in the Busan area. As it rose to a crisis level Park Chung Hee was assassinated by the head of the KCIA, who objected to the president's decision to suppress the protesters rather than negotiate with them. A brief period of political liberation, sometimes referred to as the 'Seoul Spring', was followed by the reassertion of South Korea's security state under General Chun Doo Hwan (Chŏn Tuhwan) in 1980. Chun's consolidation of power was accompanied by the brutal suppression of a popular insurrection in the south-western city of Kwangju. This Kwangju Incident would go on to haunt the Chun regime, which remained unpopular and 'illegitimate' to many Koreans. Chun continued with Park policies, with, at first, only some cosmetic changes. The nightly curfews and the standing at attention at 5 p.m. came to an end and students no longer wore military uniforms. However, from the mid-1980s the government reduced censorship and eased its harassment of political dissidents. South Korea in the 1980s was no longer moving in an authoritarian direction. Meanwhile, its economy continued to advance in the fast track.

While all this was happening the standard of living for most South Koreans improved considerably. In 1960, South Korean per capita income was the same as Haiti, a little lower than Ghana. A decade later it was much higher, although perhaps no more so than in North Korea. By the 1980s South Korean living standards had so dramatically improved that no one would think of comparing them with Haiti or Ghana. And by almost any measure of well-being, the vast majority were better off than most North Koreans. They were far better fed, better educated, healthier, living in more spacious modern housing, and had greater access to recreation and entertainment. The squalor that characterized southern cities with their beggars, children selling gum, dirty streets, and shabbily dressed poor had largely disappeared by then. One thing South Koreans shared with their compatriots in the North was the long hours they toiled. South Koreans did not have to do many hours of 'volunteer' labour or attend lengthy, compulsory 'study sessions' (see below) but at their company or organization they put in fifty or sixty hours a week. In fact, in the 1970s and 1980s, they worked more hours than those of any country where such records were available. Working conditions were often grim and dangerous. Young women often lived in 'beehives'—tiny dormitories at work. The industrial accident rate was among the highest in the world. While living standards were improving, life was still hard and many South Koreans in the 1970s and 1980s emigrated abroad. Those who stayed at home were becoming increasingly restless.

North Korea: losing economic momentum, becoming a dynastic state

The North moved in its own eccentric direction in the 1970s and 1980s, evolving into a dynastic cult state, whose ideology became further removed from orthodox Marxism-Leninism. When Mao Zedong carried out his Cultural Revolution beginning in 1966, Kim followed with his less chaotic version. State propaganda praised him as a greater thinker. His *juche* (*chuch'e*) thought, a term often translated as 'self-reliance', became the ideological foundation of society. In 1972, a new constitution was promulgated to replace the one drawn up by the Soviets in 1948. It declared *juche*, 'an adoption of socialism to Korea', as the basis of the government. After the 1970s references to Marxism-Leninism disappeared. A great tower of *juche* thought was erected in the capital whose red flame stood out in the night skyline. North Koreans were required to study Kim Il Sung's thought in weekly, semi-weekly, and even daily study sessions at their workplace. The state spent scarce foreign exchange buying pages in foreign newspapers extolling the great leader and his thought, and sponsoring Juche Study Societies overseas. Meanwhile, Kim's cult of personality, originally modelled on Stalin's, reached proportions so extreme as to strike even sympathetic foreign observers as bizarre. His portraits and statues were everywhere, his quotations were carved in giant letters on the mountainsides. From the early 1970s all citizens were required to wear a badge with his image.

A distinctive feature of the cult of Kim Il Sung that set it apart from other communist states was that it was extended to his family. His mother, father, great-great grandfather, and his first wife all became objects of patriotic devotion. This had been true from the early days of the regime but a heightened emphasis on his 'revolutionary lineage' in the 1970s coincided with the emergence of his son Kim Jong Il as his designated successor. This was done quietly at first: Kim Jong Il never appeared in public and was unknown outside the Party elite. Then in 1980, Kim Jong Il made his public debut at the Korean Workers' Party Congress. Thereafter, he was shown on television and in the press accompanied by his father. His picture too appeared everywhere, and the younger Kim began to receive the adulation previously reserved for his father. North Korea had become a dynastic state.

Not only was the Kim family portrayed at the centre of the Korean nation, Pyongyang became its geographic centre. Previously, the North was the base camp from which the unfinished nationalist struggle for liberation would continue until the imperialists were driven out of the South and the country's unity restored. The 1972 constitution declared Pyongyang not Seoul the nation's capital. A new Pyongyang-centred nationalism was emerging. In the early 1990s, archaeologists, at the suggestion of Kim Il Sung, discovered an ancient civilization based at Pyongyang, which was proclaimed the cradle of Korean culture.

While the ideology evolved, economic policies remained frozen in the early years of the regime. Unlike most communist states that made some concessions to private markets, the DPRK maintained total state control over the economy. Lacking the foreign exchange to import technology, the regime simply tried to apply more labour to meet production goals. Soldiers devoted much of their time to construction projects and helping to harvest crops. Students spent as many days labouring in the fields and at construction sites as in school, and government offices were closed on Fridays so that all employees could do 'volunteer' labour. The state organized 'speed battles' to meet unrealistically high targets, which were almost always falsely declared successful. North Korean workers and farmers were bombarded with exhortations to inspire them as they toiled at weekends and after work. The same methods, however, resulted in diminishing returns. It is difficult to determine growth rates in North Korea where even basic statistics are kept secret, but its economic growth after the early 1970s appeared to have slowed down. In the 1980s, it was barely growing at all.

What little economic growth it achieved in the 1980s was in good part due to aid from the Soviet Union, including the supply of petroleum at well below the market price. Still the DPRK found itself desperately short of foreign exchange since it produced little that anyone wanted. As a result, the state began to resort to criminal activity to raise foreign exchange. It produced narcotics delivered by its diplomats in their pouches, exported counterfeit cigarettes, printed counterfeit US currency, and engaged in arms smuggling.

The contrast with South Korea could not be greater. While the ROK in the 1980s was becoming an export powerhouse selling electronics, appliances, steel, ships, and textiles, North Korea was engaged in illegal enterprises to earn even modest amounts of foreign exchange. While the ROK's economic growth was accelerating in the 1980s, the DPRK economy was stagnant. While in South Korea living standards were rising sharply, North Koreans after 1980 were experiencing serious food shortages and malnutrition. In the economic competition between the two Koreas, South Korea was clearly winning.

Chapter 6
Globalizing south, inward north

From the 1980s the two Koreas grew further apart, economically, politically, and culturally. As they did each became an outlier in the history of post-colonial states. Few states moved faster from poverty to 'developed' status than South Korea, none developed a more totalitarian, isolated society than North Korea. South Korea's economy expanded impressively well into the 2000s, becoming a wealthy consumer society, while North Korea went through economic stagnation, decline, and the worst famine any urban society has ever experienced. Both started with authoritarian political systems; however, the South evolved into an open, democratic society while the North remained authoritarian and closed. The South became a cosmopolitan society with a globe-trotting population, internationally recognized brand companies, and a globally popular entertainment industry. The North became increasingly inward-looking, moving from a more conventional Marxist-Leninist state that placed itself within an international socialist movement to a dynastic cult state based on a xenophobic racial-nationalism.

Most Koreans continued to see themselves as part of one nation united by common ethnicity and ancestry, and they regarded the political division as unnatural and in the long term unacceptable. Yet by the second decade of the 21st century it was not certain when or if reunification would occur; nor was it clear to what extent the two Koreas were still one nation.

A dramatic reversal of fortunes in the late 1980s and early 1990s

In 1981, following a recession that accompanied the chaotic period between the death of Park Chung Hee and Chun Doo Hwan's consolidation of power, South Korea returned to fast economic growth led by surging exports. That same year it was awarded the 1988 Olympic Games, which acted as an impetus for infrastructural development. Over the next few years its economic growth rates reached 12 per cent, the highest in the world. Developing nations began to admire its achievements and sent a steady stream of observers to learn from it. The ROK was becoming the poster child for successful economic development; journalists outside the country were referring to the 'Korean economic miracle'. But the miracle came at the price of labour suppression, long hours, and low wages. Student and labour unrest only became greater during the decade, joined by an increasingly restless middle class that resented being excluded from political participation.

In 1987 massive anti-government demonstrations broke out when the government announced that although Chun would step down as he promised at the end of his seven-year term, there would be no direct elections for a new president. It was clear Chun would simply pick another general to succeed him. Protest demonstrations became so frequent and massive that they jeopardized the Olympic Games. In June 1987, the government, responding to escalating public pressure, promised a freely contested presidential election and ended most censorship. It released most political prisoners. An election at the end of that year was won by the very candidate Chun had picked against a fractured opposition, but opposition parties soon gained a large majority in the National Assembly. Politics became more open with a lively press, organized interest groups, and freely contested elections at all levels. The military completely withdrew from politics. In 1992, a former opposition politician, Kim Young Sam (Kim Yŏngsam), was elected president. In 1997, another former opponent of the Park and Chun regimes, Kim Dae Jung, was elected. By then peaceful transfers of power were already becoming routine.

A wave of labour unrest was unleashed in 1987, as workers could now freely organize. Over the next few years wages rose rapidly, and working conditions and safety standards improved considerably. The standard of living rose dramatically, and South Korea became a modern consumer society. The streets were soon clogged with cars and the stores filled with products from around the world as import restrictions eased. After 1988, almost all restrictions on travel abroad ended and soon South Koreans became among the world's busiest globetrotters. In the 1990s, the middle-class consumer lifestyle was becoming within reach of the average working family; the gap in living standards between them and their counterparts in the First World nations narrowed. In 1996, South Korea joined the OECD, an organization of developed nations, symbolically graduating from Third to First World status.

All this was a dramatic contrast with the economic stagnation of North Korea. In the early 1980s, Kim Il Sung, his son and designated successor Kim Jong Il, as well as other officials, travelled to China to learn about that country's economic reforms. A few modest gestures toward opening up the country to foreign investment were carried out. Yet, rather than reform, the regime conducted more mass mobilization campaigns, using the same methods it had been employing since the 1950s to spur economic growth. It also sought more aid from the Soviet Union which Moscow, concerned about its waning influence in Asia, provided. Internally, there was no loosening of the tight grip the state maintained over society.

Even more alarming to Pyongyang than its southern rival's economic success was its growing international recognition. As many developing countries began to see the South as the more useful model to learn from and as a source of trade and economic aid, Pyongyang's influence in the Third World waned. The DPRK's abuse of diplomatic privilege to engage in drug smuggling, its sponsorship of terrorist attacks on South Korea, the extreme cult of Kim Il Sung, and the promotion of his son as his successor made the Non-Aligned nations increasingly weary of the DPRK. After 1982, they ceased to put forward pro-DPRK resolutions at the UN. The Olympic Games were another challenge. First Pyongyang tried to discourage countries from attending by carrying out several terrorist attacks and spreading rumours that the ROK was plagued with the AIDS epidemic. It then insisted on co-hosting the games. When it was offered the opportunity to host a few minor events Pyongyang rejected it and then campaigned for an international boycott. Only five countries joined the boycott; the games were well attended and successful.

The biggest threat to Pyongyang was the thaw in relations between its communist allies and the government in Seoul. China, the Soviet Union, and the Warsaw Pact nations of Eastern Europe sent training teams to the ROK and began inviting the South Koreans to sporting events in their countries. Hungary opened full diplomatic relations with Seoul in 1988, and the Soviet Union did so in 1990. Moscow's establishment of official relations with South Korea was accompanied by the end of its economic aid to the North. Just how important Soviet aid was became apparent when its suspension resulted in a serious contraction of the DPRK economy. An especially hard blow was Moscow's insistence that Pyongyang pay market prices for its petroleum with foreign exchange. North Korea had relied on cheap Soviet oil to run its economy. It now suffered from severe energy shortages resulting in power outages, plants closing, and idle trains, trucks, and tractors. Fertilizer production fell, adversely impacting agricultural production. The South Korean government sought to

utilize the changing international dynamics by proposing new
talks with North Korea. After negotiations the two agreed on a
nuclear-free peninsula but otherwise little progress was made.

North Korea's 'arduous march'

By the early 1990s the character of the nearly half-century
of rivalry between the two Koreas had changed. North Korea was
no longer a serious rival, rather it was verging on being a failed
state. Its leadership, without abandoning its official goal of
reunification, became more focused on survival. Many
South Koreans as well as outside observers expected the
North Korean state to collapse and to be annexed by its more
populous, far wealthier southern neighbour, much as East
Germany had become incorporated into West Germany. Indeed,
rather than worry about a North Korean invasion or political
subversion, leaders in Seoul fretted about the cost of absorbing
the North when its inevitable collapse came.

By the start of 1994, economic conditions in the North had
deteriorated to the point that Kim Il Sung in his annual New Year's
address for the first time admitted things were not going well.
In the coming months North Korea narrowly averted a conflict
with the United States over its nuclear programme. In tense
last-minute negotiations Pyongyang agreed to halt its nuclear
weapons development in return for US, South Korean, and
Japanese assistance in building two nuclear power plants and
providing heavy fuel oil. The details were still being worked out
when Kim died suddenly in July 1994. His son Kim Jong Il, as had
long been planned, succeeded him.

The following summer unusually heavy monsoon rains brought
about widespread flooding, the loss of much of the nation's
harvest, and famine. From 1995 to 1999 hundreds of thousands
of North Koreans died of causes related to malnutrition in one of
the late 20th century's worst famines. The North Korea famine,

or 'arduous march' as it was called, was a truly unusual event in world history. It was the first ever in a modern urban, industrial society that was not at war. Unlike other famines that mainly affected rural areas this hit the industrial cities of the north-east the hardest. Desperate, Kim Jong Il called on international food aid. His response was in some ways remarkable. In a country still claiming to be a paradise on earth, a model for other nations, a self-reliant state, the admission of the famine and the urgent call for mass assistance was striking. It was also a major risk to the regime.

Ordinary North Koreans had no contact with the outside world. They were told that they were the envy of their neighbours, and that their South Korean brothers and sisters were suffering from endless repression by the American imperialists and their southern lackeys. Yet, the narrative went, the spirits of the people of the South were kept up by the hope and expectation that they would be liberated one day by the DPRK and live under the brilliant Kim family. The regime now risked exposing their people to alternative views of reality which could undermine its legitimacy. Relief workers from the US, the UN World Food Program, and private NGOs including the Good Friends organization in South Korea delivered food. They were severely restricted in their movements, their contact with ordinary North Koreans was limited, but nonetheless millions of people were knowingly being fed by their 'enemies'.

Despite these setbacks, the North Korean regime did not, as some expected, collapse but survived. It did this by modifying its ideology, adjusting some of its political institutions, and adapting to economic and social changes. Many of the ideological changes were already under way before the economic freefall and famine. They included taking a more ultra-nationalist turn. When in the late 1980s North Korea began to find itself in a changing international environment in which its very survival was at stake it responded by re-emphasizing ethnic-racial nationalism. It still called itself socialist but 'socialist in our own style'. In effect it was withdrawing from the declining international socialist movement and retreating into xenophobic isolationism.

The regime revived some cultural traditions such as celebrating the autumn moon festival and lunar New Year. State propaganda placed more emphasis on the uniqueness not only of Korean culture but of the Korean race or bloodline. Tan'gun, the mythical founder of Korea, previously regarded as in the realm of folklore, became a real historical person. In 1993, his grave was discovered. Other discoveries included early human remains that 'proved' Koreans were a unique line of human evolution. This was part of a larger narrative in which all of Korean history was reinterpreted as the struggle of Koreans to maintain their independence, their own march of progress, and their racial purity in the face of foreign invaders. Fortunately, the remarkable Kim family had come along and, under their leadership, half the nation had liberated itself from Japanese rule, and had thwarted an American attempt to subdue them. The DPRK under its powerful military and inspired leadership was keeping the imperialists at bay until the time it could liberate the other half of the nation.

While elements of this narrative had existed since the early days of the regime, it now became the central story, the justification for the regime and the explanation for its hardships. The famine itself, a product of overly centralized state-directed agriculture, deforestation, and ill-conceived farming practices, was blamed on the sanctions imposed by the imperialist powers. The regime could take credit for forcing foreigners to relieve the famine that they were, in good measure, responsible for. Furthermore, unable to point to economic progress, the regime pointed to its military achievements. This led to a shift away from focusing on economic progress in state propaganda to military progress. Kim Jong Il in 1998 adopted a 'military first' policy giving greater visibility to its armed forces and highlighting the need for military strength to confront the threats from foreign imperialists. That year the constitution was amended to make the National Defence

Commission the highest organ of the state. Military men were appointed to key positions.

Kim Jong Il's government also adapted to the changing reality of economic collapse. Prior to the famine, most people received their food and other basic material needs through a public distribution system, but this broke down. Instead most North Koreans had begun to rely on private markets to purchase food. Once prohibited, these were tolerated and then openly permitted. In 2002, the state shifted to a more money-based economy, charging market prices for rent and other state-provided goods and services, simultaneously increasing salaries so that employees could pay for them. It allowed and even encouraged state institutions to engage in market activities to raise their own funds. State enterprises and private traders were permitted to cross the border with China to engage in trade. The state, however, never fully embraced the private market and placed restrictions on it; and it continued to call itself socialist. But in practice, in the decade following the famine North Korea developed a mixed economy. This was more an acceptance of the reality that most families and institutions were fending for themselves to survive than it was an enthusiastic bout of reform. In fact, what kinds of market activities were permitted or tolerated by the state was not clear, and subject to change. Still, incomplete, grudging, and inconsistent as state economic policies were, they enabled the North Korean people and the state to muddle through.

While North Korea was coping with its economic crisis, South Korean president Kim Dae Jung sought to improve relations with North Korea in what he called his 'Sunshine Policy'. This offered friendly exchanges and economic assistance to the DPRK in return for an end to hostilities. The hope was to gradually bring the two Koreas closer together. In 2000, he went to Pyongyang for a summit conference with Kim Jong Il. This was followed by some limited trade. In 2002, the Hyundai Corporation of South Korea opened a tourist resort for South Koreans in the famed Diamond (Kŭmgang) Mountains of North Korea. Two years later, the two governments set up the Kaesong Industrial Complex a few miles into the DPRK. South Korean firms were given tax incentives to open businesses there. Seven years later nearly 50,000 North Korean workers were employed by some 100 southern firms. Meanwhile, Seoul provided some food and other aid; and there were some cultural exchanges.

However, the economic benefits for North Korea, always searching for foreign exchange, had to be balanced by the need to limit contact between its citizens and the people of the South. Furthermore, the explanation for economic setbacks, and the rationale for military spending and need for absolute loyalty to the ruling Kim family all required a continual threat of foreign invasion. Periods of modest cooperation therefore alternated with crises, mostly manufactured by Pyongyang. One excuse was the joint military exercises by US and South Korean troops. The North Korean regime complained that these were rehearsals for an invasion, a claim primarily intended to remind their own people of the foreign menace but also to use as leverage in negotiations with Seoul and Washington. In 2008, for example, on the same day the South Korean president Lee Myung-bak (Yi Myŏngbak) was announcing a plan to help develop the North Korean economy, a DPRK guard shot dead a South Korean tourist at the Diamond Mountain resort who had strayed outside the permitted zone. Seoul then prohibited tourists from going there. In March 2010 a DPRK torpedo sank the South Korean destroyer *Cheonan (Chŏnan)*, killing forty-five sailors. In November that year, DPRK artillery shelled the South Korean island of Yŏnp'yŏng resulting in several deaths. The most provocative acts involved testing missiles and detonating nuclear bombs. In 1998, Pyongyang fired a medium-range missile over Japan. In 2006, in violation of its denuclearization agreement with the ROK, it tested a small nuclear device. It tested a larger one in 2009.

Although it allowed more market activity, and widespread corruption made the state less efficient at enforcing all rules and restrictions, there was no attempt at liberalizing the regime. Indoctrination campaigns continued and radio receivers were checked to make sure they were not able to receive any but DPRK state channels. Midnight inspections checked homes to make sure there were no unauthorized reading materials. Perhaps 200,000 political prisoners toiled away at hard labour in remote camps. But it was becoming increasingly difficult to wall off all information about the outside world. Traders from China smuggled in South Korean videos, which were immensely popular. Young North Koreans became familiar with South Korean pop singers and a few even adopted South Korean hairstyles. Yet there was no sign of any organized opposition.

South Korea: democratization and globalization

The Olympic Games of 1988 were a kind of coming out party for South Korea. They were used by Seoul to showcase the country's emergence as a modern industrial nation. The ROK was also an increasingly democratic one as exemplified by the election of Kim Dae Jung as president in 1997. No opposition leader was more hated by the military rulers. He narrowly escaped execution twice, by Park in 1973 and by Chun in 1980, saved only by the intervention of the United States. But his narrow victory went uncontested and was accepted as a matter of course. Two basic political groupings—a more conservative and a more liberal one—alternated in power over the next two decades, both of which shared broad agreement on many issues. One healthy sign of political pluralism was the rise of NGOs advocating government transparency, women's rights, environmental protection, and other interests and issues. A lively media that included investigative reporting also acted as a watchdog on the government as well as on the corporate world.

There were some limits on free speech, most notably the National Security Law, which every administration promised to repeal but each found useful. Aimed at curbing North Korean subversion it was interpreted more broadly to stifle dissent. A major problem in creating an open, transparent, and accountable society was corruption. Every president after 1987 ended up being implicated or having family members implicated in financial scandals ranging from bribery to influence peddling. The most shocking case was Park Geun-hye (Pak Kŭnhye), daughter of the former dictator Park Chung Hee, elected by the conservative party in a typically close election in 2012. In the wake of bribery and influence peddling by her long-term confidant, she was forced to resign in 2017 after massive protests and the loss of support among her own party. Despite the National Security Law, its scandals, and its frequent demonstrations, South Korea was, along with India, Japan, and Taiwan, the most transparent and democratic society in Asia.

South Korea's economy went through an economic crisis in 1997–8, part of a wider Asian economic turmoil that began in Thailand. In 1998, its economy contracted 5.8 per cent and it had to receive a massive bailout by the IMF, one of the largest ever given. But it soon recovered, resumed high rates of growth, and paid off massive foreign loans in just three years. In fact, in the 2000s it went from chronic trade deficits to large surpluses, from a debtor to a creditor country. After 2008, the economy slowed to a 3 per cent annual growth rate, which the public and the state found worrisome but was still slightly above the average for developed nations. By 2018, its GDP per capita was on a par with the EU nations, a little above Italy, a little below Britain and France. By that time, by any measure it was a prosperous First World nation.

South Korea had been remarkably successful at keeping up with technology. By the 2010s it ranked fifth or sixth in the world in the number of patents issued, and it was a leader in developing innovative consumer electronics products. Its goods were acquiring a reputation for high quality. However, it faced stiff competition from a rising China. China after 2005 replaced the USA as South Korea's largest trading partner. Unlike most countries South Korea generally ran a trade surplus with Beijing. But by the 2010s China was beginning to outcompete Koreans in steel, ships, and other major export sectors. It seemed a matter of time before it was able to compete in more advanced technology. Meanwhile, the shift from a manufacturing to a knowledge-based and service-based economy was occurring much more slowly than most economists thought desirable.

With its highly developed, often state-of-the-art infrastructure, modern high rises, and highways, South Korea was to all appearances a wealthy country by the second decade of the 21st century. Even in the countryside most families had nice modern homes and were serviced by good roads. It had become the most wired country in the world, with almost universal access to high speed internet. Yet income distribution, which had been one of the most equal in the developing world, began to become more unequal. The unemployment rate, lower than average for developed countries, was creeping higher. The country had a weak safety net. Social welfare programmes expanded after 1998 yet remained below the level of most advanced economies. Poverty among the elderly was becoming a problem.

Besides a growing economic inequality, South Korea made only modest progress in addressing gender inequality. In contrast to North Korea's progressive laws on women, South Korea in the 1950s passed a Family Law that reinforced the traditional hierarchical nature of society. Men headed households, almost always gained custody of children in divorce, and the latter was extremely difficult for women to obtain. After 1987, the Family Law was reformed to create greater gender equality and in the early 2000s legislation was passed prohibiting all sorts of gender discrimination. Still, Korean women lagged behind their counterparts in almost all other developed countries and in many developing countries in their representation in government and the professions, and until after 2000 in higher education. Some things did change, such as divorce rates which more than doubled between 1995 and 2005 and by 2010 had reached European and Japanese levels. Being a single mother, however, was difficult due to continued discrimination against women in the workplace, despite laws against it.

One of the problems of South Korean society was the concentration of wealth and influence in the *chaebŏl*s. Once closely dependent on the state, by the 1990s the *chaebŏl*s had become 'too big to fail'. That is, the state could no longer discipline them without endangering the whole economy. The 1997–8 financial crisis presented an opportunity to control their overexpansion. A few such as Daewoo were forced into bankruptcy; others were restructured to focus more on their core areas. But the quick recovery brought these limited reforms to a halt. The surviving *chaebŏl*s such as Lotte, Hyundai, Ssangyong, and Samsung only became bigger. Samsung, in particular, which in 2017 became the world's largest privately traded firm by sales volume, had an enormous influence over the country's economy. Since the founding families still had controlling shares in most of these conglomerates, their influence was enormous. Sons and daughters of *chaebŏl* families often married the offspring of other *chaebŏl* founders, creating a small interrelated class reminiscent of the elite families that dominated dynastic Korea or of the intermarried elite of North Korea. Calls for the reining in of these powerful firms and their families became a major political issue in the 2010s.

Few achievements were more outstanding than in education. In 1945, only 5 per cent of Koreans had a secondary education; half had no formal education at all. By the early 20th century South Korea had become one of the world's most literate nations. In the 2010s it ranked second or third in the number of people under 35 with a university degree. South Korean secondary students consistently ranked at or near the top in international comparative tests of maths, science, reading, and analytical skills. Yet, although much admired, it was a costly, inefficient, hyper-competitive system that reduced schooling to test-preparation, drove families to spend large sums on cramming schools and private tutoring, and placed enormous stress on young people. By some measures South Korean families spent a higher percentage of their income and students put in longer hours on education than in any other society. Another issue was the quality of higher education. For all its often-praised achievements in schooling few of its universities ranked in the top 100. While many company laboratories produced patent-protected products and processes, not a single Korean scientist had as of 2018 won a Nobel Prize.

The cost of education in both resources and time contributed to another major problem, the low birth rate. While South Korea's high birth rate resulted in a vigorous state-sponsored family planning effort in the 1960s, by the start of the 21st century officials worried that women were having too few babies. In the 2010s that birth rate had fallen to under 1.2 children per woman, and was the second lowest in the world, significantly lower than in Japan. The population, which had reached fifty million by 2018, was expected to decline sharply from 2030. The reasons for this remarkable development are varied. Besides the cost of educating children, many younger women were quietly rebelling against the expectations most men had that they devote themselves to their husbands and children after marriage. Many women were putting off marriage until quite late and some were opting out of marriage altogether. Meanwhile, improvements in health resulted in South Koreans having among the world's longest life spans. Consequently, the country was likely to become an extreme case of an ageing society.

To deal with the impending labour shortage, the government instituted some pro-natal policies, but these were ineffective. Another solution was immigration. Several hundred thousand immigrants from China, the Philippines, Mongolia, Bangladesh, Nepal, and other Asian countries were employed legally under short- or medium-term contracts doing jobs that were dirty, dangerous, and difficult. But they were expected to return to their home countries after their term of employment was over. An ethnically homogeneous people that except for the Japanese colonists had not experienced an influx of immigrants in centuries, most Koreans were not comfortable with the idea of permanent immigration. Yet many experts argued that immigration was needed if the country wanted to avoid a severe demographic crisis in the future.

Continuous crisis

When Kim Jong Un (Kim Chŏngŭn) succeeded his father as North Korean leader in December 2011, many in South Korea and the international community hoped for a change in the direction of the country (Figure 10). Kim had been educated at private school in Switzerland, was young, not yet 30, and thought to be more open to new ideas, more cosmopolitan than his father or grandfather. However, in the spring of 2013, Kim manufactured another crisis, claiming the routine annual joint military exercises between US and ROK forces were a dangerous provocation. His anti-Seoul and Washington rhetoric went beyond anything previously from the DPRK: declaring the country was at a 'state of war' he threatened to turn Seoul into a 'sea of fire'. Pyongyang cancelled the non-aggression pacts previously signed with South Korea, closed the border crossing, disconnected the hotline that had been established with Seoul, and shut down the Kaesong Industrial Complex. Tensions eased but relations between North and South were at a low point.

Kim Jong Un carried out the consolidation of power with unprecedented ruthlessness. Many top military and civilian leaders were purged. In December 2013, he murdered his uncle Chang Sŏngt'aek, considered the number two person in the regime, having him publicly arrested and then executed. In February 2017 North Korean agents assassinated his half-brother Kim Jong

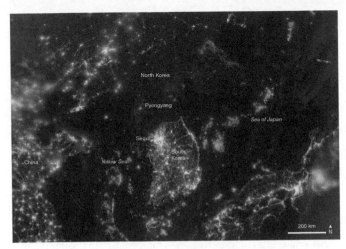

10. Satellite image of the Korean peninsula at night, 24 September 2012.

Nam at Kuala Lumpur airport. Not only was this killing of a member of the immediate Kim family unprecedented, it was carried out despite the fact he was living in exile in Beijing under Chinese protection. At home, Kim Jong Un tightened border security, making it more difficult for those trying to flee the country. Nor was there economic liberalization. In May 2016, Kim held the first party congress since 1980. The 2016 Congress was used to revive many of the old party institutions from Kim Il Sung's days in power. It also revived the use of fixed-year development plans that had been abandoned in the early 1990s by issuing a new Five-Year Plan. None of this suggested radical change.

To the dismay of most South Koreans as well as their American allies and their Chinese and Japanese neighbours, Kim Jong Un accelerated his missile and nuclear programmes. He conducted two nuclear tests in 2016 that resulted in new rounds of economic sanctions. Despite universal condemnation and the UN sanctions North Korea carried out a nuclear test in September 2017 that was far larger than previous ones, possibly a hydrogen bomb. In July

2017 it tested two intercontinental missiles capable of reaching Alaska; and in November 2017 it fired a missile capable of reaching Washington DC or anywhere in the USA. Officials in America became so alarmed that they considered the possibility of carrying out a military strike against North Korean facilities. However, the vulnerability of Seoul, only 40 km from the border, within range of DPRK artillery and rocket attacks, as well as the possibility that a military strike could lead to nuclear war, made this a rather desperate option.

In South Korea public opinion toward the North hardened, even among many younger people. Opinion polls showed that for the first time, narrow majorities of the public were open to the possible development of the country's own nuclear weapons. Yet in May 2017 South Koreans elected the liberal candidate Moon Jae-in as president, who advocated a revival of the Sunshine Policy of his liberal predecessors. Then, perhaps encouraged by the new administration in Seoul, Kim Jong Un in his 2018 New Year's address offered a more conciliatory approach. North Koreans participated in the Olympic Winter Games in South Korea in February 2018, and the two leaders had an unprecedented three summit meetings in the following six months. Even more unprecedented were the summit meetings between Kim Jong Un and US President Trump in Singapore in June 2018, in Hanoi in February 2019, and at the DMZ in June 2019. North Korea was now offering to halt its nuclear and missile programmes in return for improved relations and easing economic sanctions. While many South Koreans remained opposed to any deal with North Korea, a majority was cautiously optimistic that this time it would be different and North Korea would carry out economic reforms and begin cooperation with Seoul.

Korea: still one nation?

Events in 2018 demonstrated that hopes for reunification in South Korea were not yet dead. The younger generation was not as emotionally wedded to the idea as the older generations were but still tended to see it as inevitable. South Koreans, however, were concerned about the financial burden of absorbing the costs of rebuilding North Korea and accommodating the refugees should the DPRK collapse, as seemed possible or even likely. They often regarded North Koreans as alien, 'brainwashed' cousins who might be too different to easily assimilate. As a result, South Koreans began to think of unification as a long-term process perhaps taking several generations. Most hoped that reunification would happen after the DPRK underwent a period of economic reform, modernization, and took steps toward developing closer connections with the South.

Yet was Korea still one nation? Were the Koreans one people and with a shared tradition that were politically divided or did seven decades of separation under such different socio-political systems create two nations? The answer was not clear. North Koreans loved South Korean TV dramas and pop music, but that was true of Chinese, Japanese, Taiwanese, Vietnamese, and the public in most of Asia. By 2018, 40,000 North Korean refugees had settled in South Korea. They encountered considerable discrimination by employers and neighbours who found them lacking in initiative and worried that some might be DPRK agents. Many refugees had trouble adjusting to South Korea's hyper-competitive society and led unhappy existences. Yet others managed to assimilate and flourish.

The differences between North and South Korean society were not the only challenge to the Korean belief that they were a single, homogeneous people. South Korea was slowly becoming a multi-cultural society. The use of sonograms in the 1980s and 1990s, combined with the preference for boys, meant there was a shortage of marriage-age women. In addition many Korean women did not want to marry farmers or did not want to marry at all. So, in the early 2010s, one in seven Korean men were marrying foreign brides, mostly from China, Vietnam, Mongolia, and other Asian countries. Thus, mixed ethnic families were becoming common. Then there was also a small but growing immigrant population. As a result, some South Koreans were starting to discuss the concept of a Korean identity not based on ethnicity, but one open to people of varied cultural and racial backgrounds. Yet a public furore in 2018 over letting in a small number of political refugees from the Middle East indicated how strong the resistance to this new conceptualization of what it meant to be Korean was.

Korea had seen such radical and rapid changes since the late 19th century that its future in 2019 was not clear. Few people, if any, in 1945 or 1953 could have predicted the strange, eccentric path of North Korea's evolution. It is not clear that anyone in the 1950s had foreseen that South Korea would in sixty years become one of the world's wealthiest and most technologically advanced societies. And it would have surprised almost everyone in the 1980s that Seoul would be a global centre of popular culture thirty years later. Therefore, it would be foolhardy to predict its future course. Yet Koreans care deeply about their history. Their long tradition of historical writing, the special role given to historians in the past, and the enormous popularity of historical novels, movies, and TV dramas attest to this. So whatever changes take place in Korea, it is likely the Korean people will remain very much aware of their distinctive identity and the traditions associated with it.

Chronology

2333 BCE	Legendary founding of first Korea state by Tan'gun
108 BCE	Chinese Han Empire invades Old Chosŏn, occupies parts of northern Korea
300s CE	Emergence of the Three Kingdoms
676	Silla unifies most of the Korean peninsula
900–35	Period of Later Three Kingdoms
935	Establishment of the Koryŏ
1270–1356	Mongol period
1392	End of the Koryŏ, establishment of new Chosŏn state under the Yi dynasty
1440s	Invention of *Hangul*, current boundaries of Korea established
1592	Japanese invasion of Korea
1644	Korea becomes tributary of Qing Dynasty China
1876	Japan 'opens' Korea
1897	The Great Han Empire proclaimed
1910–45	Japanese colonial period
1919	March First Movement
1945	USA and Soviet Union divide Korea into occupation zones along 38th parallel
1948	Republic of Korea and the Democratic People's Republic of Korea proclaimed

1950–3	Korean War
1961	South Korea begins 'economic take-off' under Park Chung Hee
1980s	North Korea enters economic stagnation then decline
1987	South Korea's transition to democracy begins
1995–9	North Korean famine
1996	South Korea reclassified as a 'developed' economy by World Bank
2006	North Korea becomes nuclear power; South Korea's 'Korean Wave' under way

Further reading

General history

Hwang, Kyung Moon. *A History of Korea*. New York: Palgrave Macmillan, 2010.

Lee, Injae, Owen Miller, Jinhoon Park, Yi Hyun-Hae, and Michael D. Shin, eds. *Korean History in Maps: From Prehistory to the Twenty-First Century*. Cambridge: Cambridge University Press, 2014.

Lee, Peter, William Theodore de Bary, Yongho Ch'oe, and Hugh H. W. King, eds. *Sources of Korean Tradition*, Vol. 1: *From Earliest Times to the Sixteenth Century*. New York: Columbia University Press, 1997.

Lee, Peter, William Theodore de Bary, and Yongho Ch'oe, eds. *Sources of Korean Tradition*, Vol. 2: *From the Sixteenth to the Twentieth Centuries*. New York: Columbia University Press, 2000.

Pratt, Keith. *Everlasting Flower: A History of Korea*. London: Reaktion Books, 2006.

Pratt, Keith, and Richard Rutt. *Korea: A Historical and Cultural Dictionary*. Richmond: Curzon Press, 1999.

Seth, Michael J. *A Concise History of Korea: From Antiquity to the Present*. 3rd edn. Lanham, Md: Rowman & Littlefield, 2020.

Pre-modern Korea

Baker, Don, and Franklin Rausch. *Catholics and Anti-Catholicism in Chosŏn Korea*. Honolulu: University of Hawaii Press, 2017.

Breuker, Remco E. *Establishing a Pluralist Society in Medieval Korea, 918–1170: History, Ideology, and Identity in the Koryo Dynasty.* Leiden: Brill, 2010.

Buzo, Adrian, and Tony Prince, trans. *Kyunyo-Jon: The Life, Times and Songs of a Tenth Century Korean Monk.* Sidney: Wild Peony Press, 1994.

De Bary, William Theodore, and JaHyun Kim Haboush, eds. *The Rise of Neo-Confucianism in Korea.* New York: Columbia University Press, 1985.

Deuchler, Martina. *The Confucian Transformation of Korea: A Study of Society and Ideology.* Cambridge, Mass.: Council on East Asian Studies, Harvard University, 1992.

Duncan, John B. *The Origins of the Chosŏn Dynasty.* Seattle: University of Washington Press, 2000.

Griffis, William Eliot. *Corea: The Hermit Nation.* 9th edn. New York: AMS Press, 1971.

Haboush, JaHyun Kim. *A Heritage of Kings: One Man's Monarchy in the Confucian World.* New York: Columbia University Press, 1988.

Haboush, JaHyun Kim. *Epistolary Korea: Letters in the Communicative Space of the Chosŏn, 1392–1910.* New York: Columbia University Press, 2009.

Haboush, JaHyun Kim. *The Memoirs of Lady Hyegyŏng: The Autobiographical Writings of a Crown Princess of Eighteenth-Century Korea.* Translated and with an Introduction and Annotations by JaHyun Kim Haboush. Berkeley: University of California Press, 1996.

Kim, Kichung. *Classical Korean Literature.* Armonk, NY: M. E. Sharpe, 1996.

Lee, Soyoung. *Korean Painting.* Oxford: Oxford University Press, 1996.

Palais, James B. *Confucian Statecraft and Korean Institutions: Yu Hyŏngwŏn and the Late Chosŏn Dynasty.* Seattle: University of Washington Press, 1996.

Shultz, Edward J. *Generals and Scholars: Military Rule in Medieval Korea.* Honolulu: University of Hawaii Press, 2000.

Xu Jing. *A Chinese Traveler in Medieval Korea: Xu Jing's Illustrated Account of the Xuanhe Embassy to Koryŏ.* Translated, Annotated, and with Introduction by Sem Vermeersch. Honolulu: University of Hawaii Press, 2016.

Armstrong, Charles K. *The North Korean Revolution, 1945–1950*. Ithaca, NY: Cornell University Press, 2003.

Armstrong, Charles K. *Tyranny of the Weak: North Korea and the World, 1950–1992*. Ithaca, NY: Cornell University Press, 2013.

Brazinsky, Gregg. *Nation Building in South Korea: Koreans, Americans, and the Making of Democracy*. Chapel Hill: University of North Carolina Press, 2007.

Buzo, Adrian. *The Politics and Leadership in North Korea*. 2nd edn. London: Routledge, 2017.

Cumings, Bruce. *Korea's Place in the Sun: A Modern History*. Updated edn. New York: W. W. Norton and Company, 2005.

Cumings, Bruce. *The Origins of the Korean War*, Vol. 1: *Liberation and the Emergence of Separate Regimes, 1945–1947*. Princeton: Princeton University Press, 1981.

Cumings, Bruce. *The Origins of the Korean War*, Vol. 2: *The Roaring of the Cataract, 1947–1950*. Princeton: Princeton University Press, 1990.

Deuchler, Martina. *Confucian Gentlemen and Barbarian Envoys: The Opening of Korea, 1875–1885*. Seattle: University of Washington Press, 1977.

Eckert, Carter J. *Offspring of Empire: The Koch'ang Kims and the Origins of Korean Capitalism*. Seattle: University of Washington Press, 1991.

Jager, Sheila Miyoshi. *Brothers at War: The Unending Conflict in Korea*. New York: W. W. Norton, 2013.

Kim, Charles R. *Youth for Nation: Culture and Protest in Cold War South Korea*. New York: Columbia University Press, 2018.

Kim, Richard. *Lost Names: Scenes from a Korean Boyhood*. Berkeley: University of California Press, 1998.

Kim, Suzy. *Everyday Life in the North Korean Revolution., 1945–1950*. Ithaca, NY: Cornell University Press, 2013.

Lankov, Andrei. *The Real North Korea: Life and Politics in the Failed Stalinist Utopia*. Oxford: Oxford University Press, 2013.

Larsen, Kirk W. *Tradition, Treaties, and Trade: Qing Imperialism and Chosŏn Korea, 1850–1910*. Cambridge, Mass.: Harvard University Press, 2008.

Lie, John. *Han Unbound: The Political Economy of South Korea*. Stanford, Calif.: Stanford University Press, 1998.

Lowe, Peter. *The Origins of the Korean War*. New York: Longman, 1986.

Lynn, Hyung Gu. *Bipolar Orders: The Two Koreas Since 1989*. Halifax, NS: Fenwood, 2007.

Myers, Brian. *The Cleanest Race: How North Koreans See Themselves—And Why It Matters*. Brooklyn, NY: Melville House, 2010.

Natsios, Andrew S. *The Great North Korean Famine*. Washington, DC: United States Institute of Peace Press, 2001.

Park, Chung Hee. *The Country, the Revolution and I*. Seoul: Hollym Corporation, 1970.

Park, Yeomi. *In Order to Live*. New York: Pengiun, 2015.

Robinson, Michael E. *Cultural Nationalism in Colonial Korea, 1920–1925*. Seattle: University of Washington Press, 1988.

Robinson, Michael E. *Korea's Twentieth-Century Odyssey*. Honolulu: University of Hawaii Press, 2007.

Seth, Michael J. *North Korea: A History*. London and New York: Palgrave Macmillan, 2018.

Seth, Michael J., ed. *Routledge Handbook of Modern Korean History*. London: Routledge, 2015.

Shin, Gi-Wook. *Ethnic Nationalism in Korea: Genealogy, Politics, and Legacy*. Stanford, Calif.: Stanford University Press, 2006.

Yoo, Theodore Jun. *The Politics of Gender in Colonial Korea: Education, Labor, and Health, 1910–1945*. Berkeley: University of California Press, 2008.

Korea

Index

For the benefit of digital users, indexed terms that span two pages (e.g., 52–53) may, on occasion, appear on only one of those pages.

Index

GEOGRAPHY
A Very Short Introduction
John A. Matthews & David T. Herbert

Modern Geography has come a long way from its historical roots in exploring foreign lands, and simply mapping and naming the regions of the world. Spanning both physical and human Geography, the discipline today is unique as a subject which can bridge the divide between the sciences and the humanities, and between the environment and our society. Using wide-ranging examples from global warming and oil, to urbanization and ethnicity, this *Very Short Introduction* paints a broad picture of the current state of Geography, its subject matter, concepts and methods, and its strengths and controversies. The book's conclusion is no less than a manifesto for Geography' future.

'Matthews and Herbert's book is written- as befits the VSI series- in an accessible prose style and is peppered with attractive and understandable images, graphs and tables.'

Geographical.

www.oup.com/vsi

GEOPOLITICS
A Very Short Introduction
Klaus Dodds

In certain places such as Iraq or Lebanon, moving a few feet either side of a territorial boundary can be a matter of life or death, dramatically highlighting the connections between place and politics. For a country's location and size as well as its sovereignty and resources all affect how the people that live there understand and interact with the wider world. Using wide-ranging examples, from historical maps to James Bond films and the rhetoric of political leaders like Churchill and George W. Bush, this Very Short Introduction shows why, for a full understanding of contemporary global politics, it is not just smart - it is essential - to be geopolitical.

'Engrossing study of a complex topic.'

Mick Herron, Geographical.

GLOBALIZATION
A Very Short Introduction
Manfred Steger

'Globalization' has become one of the defining buzzwords of our time - a term that describes a variety of accelerating economic, political, cultural, ideological, and environmental processes that are rapidly altering our experience of the world. It is by its nature a dynamic topic - and this *Very Short Introduction* has been fully updated for 2009, to include developments in global politics, the impact of terrorism, and environmental issues. Presenting globalization in accessible language as a multifaceted process encompassing global, regional, and local aspects of social life, Manfred B. Steger looks at its causes and effects, examines whether it is a new phenomenon, and explores the question of whether, ultimately, globalization is a good or a bad thing.

www.oup.com/vsi